WORK-FAMILY READY

NAVIGATING YOUR JOB WHILE PARENTING TEENS

EDITED BY
SCOTT BEHSON, Ph.D.

A READY GUIDE

PARENT READY

PARENT READY!

2025 Edition

Copyright © Parent Ready, Inc., 2025

Parent Ready supports the right to free expression and the value of copyright. The purpose of copyright is to encourage the creation of works that enrich our culture.

All rights reserved. No part of this book may be reprinted or reproduced in any form or by any electronic, mechanical, or other means, now known or hereafter invented, including photocopying, recording, and information storage and retrieval, without the prior written permission of the publisher, except in the case of brief quotations embodied in critical articles and reviews.

Published by Parent Ready, Inc.
8 East Windsor Avenue
Alexandria, Virginia 22301
https://parentready.com

Parent Ready and design are trademarks of Parent Ready, Inc.

The publisher is not responsible for websites (or their contents) that are not owned by the publisher.

ISBN: 979-8-9906505-2-7 (paperback)
ISBN: 979-8-9906505-7-2 (e-book)

Bulk purchases: Quantity discounts are available. Please make inquiries via https://workfamilyready.guide.

Table of Contents

Contributors v
Introduction by Scott Behson, Ph.D. xi

Part I. Your World Is Changing

Chapter 1: How Does Having a Teen Change You? 3
    Andy Pool, Ph.D. and Eden Pontz

Chapter 2: How Does Having a Teen Change Your Household? 15
    Brian Page, M.Ed., AFC®, Fair Play Facilitator®

Chapter 3: How Does Having a Teen Affect Your Work? 25
    Karen Clark Salinas

Part II. Strategies for Parents to Manage Work-Family Fit

Chapter 4: Setting Boundaries at Home to Accommodate Work ... 39
    Heather Cluley Bar-Or, Ph.D. and Tracy Hecht, Ph.D.

Chapter 5: Aligning with Your Co-Parent for Effective Family Management 49
    Alyssa Westring, Ph.D.

Chapter 6: Partnering with Your Teen 57
    Kelly Chandler, Ph.D.

Chapter 7: Setting Boundaries at Work to Accommodate Your Family 67
    Susan Russo

Part III. Care for Self and Others

Chapter 8: The Panini Generation: Balancing Parenting
    Teens and Other Caregiving Responsibilities 77
    Julia Beck

Chapter 9: Self-Care 87
    Andy Pool, Ph.D. and Eden Pontz

Part IV. The Role of Managers and Workplaces in Supporting Parents

Chapter 10: Creating a Family-Friendly Workplace Culture 99
    Jennifer Sabatini Fraone

Chapter 11: Manager-Employee Communication Strategies:
    Supporting Parents of Teenagers in the Workplace 109
    Amy Beacom, Ed.D.

Conclusion. 119

Contributors

Editor

Scott Behson, Ph.D., is a professor of management and Silberman Global Faculty Fellow at Fairleigh Dickinson University and a leading expert in work-life, wellness, and flexible workplaces. He's the author of three books, most recently *The Whole-Person Workplace: Building Better Workplaces Through Work-Life, Wellness, and Employee Support*—based on research, best practices, and interviews with dozens of business leaders right as they were navigating COVID changes to the workplace. His other books are *The Working Dad's Survival Guide* and *We Hate Team Projects!*

Scott is a speaker and consultant who has worked with leading companies on workplace flexibility and building supportive work cultures. He was a featured speaker at the UN's International Day of the Family and The White House's Summit for Working Families. In addition to his many academic publications, his work appears at HBR, *Time*, Fast Company, Success, WorkSpan, *WSJ*, and more. He has appeared on NBC, CBS, MSNBC, NPR, and Bloomberg Radio, as well as many leading HR and business podcasts.

Scott's favorite and most important roles are husband and father. He lives with his wife, son, and cats in Nyack, New York. Visit him online at ScottBehson.com.

Contributors

Amy Beacom, Ed.D., is credited with founding the field of parental leave coaching and consulting in 2006 after the birth of her first child through her doctoral work at Columbia University. She started the Center for Parental Leave Leadership (CPLL) in 2014 and the RETAIN Coaching Institute in 2022. She is the author of the first book to guide people through leave, *The Parental Leave Playbook*, and countless other writings. Amy has trained and certified more than 130 RETAIN Parental Leave Coaches in 36 states and 5 countries. The manager-focused training program she created can be found in more than 80 countries around the world. Amy is recognized as the United States' premier expert on the personal and professional interplay around parental leave for employers and employees.

Julia Beck, founder of the It's Working Project, has been an active and engaged industry innovator for more than 30 years. As the category's definitive elder statesman and strategic partner, Julia has been on the leading edge of the conversation about the challenges at the intersection of caregiving and the working woman. Julia coined the term "Panini Generation" as a modern metaphor to represent the pressures that Gen X and later generations struggle with as they juggle multiple responsibilities in a world that is rapidly changing socially, economically, and technologically. A mother to four adult children and two adorable dogs and wife to her all-time favorite person, Julia enjoys music, cooking, reading, travel, Pilates, and time with friends.

Kelly Chandler, Ph.D., is an associate professor in the School of Human Development and Family Sciences in the College of Health at Oregon State University. She studies the diversity in work and family experiences and the implications for relationships, health, and well-being of employees, their partners, and their children. She applies work-family justice and racial justice lenses to identify ways to reduce work-family conflict and to promote thriving at work and with family for all.

Karen Clark Salinas, Founder of Rebalance Wellbeing and Lead Coach at BetterUp, is a work-life integration strategist and National Board Certified Health & Wellness Coach. As creator of the Rebalance to Reinvent Accelerator, she guides ambitious midlife women to reclaim time, energy, and purpose—without sacrificing career momentum or family connection. Karen combines professional expertise with authentic lived experience. Her personal journey through motherhood, chronic illness, caregiving, divorce, and building a blended family shapes her compassionate yet strategic approach. She empowers high-achieving women to break free from burnout, redesign their lives around what truly matters, and lead with renewed clarity, confidence, and joy.

Heather Cluley Bar-Or, Ph.D., is the associate director of the graduate Human Resource Development program at Villanova University, overseeing curriculum, learning technology, and program outcomes for one of the school's largest graduate programs. She teaches courses on strategic human resource management, organizational behavior, and work-family and career considerations. Heather is an Integrated Life Advocate and co-leads an Overwhelmed Mitigation Group with the ThirdPath Institute. Personally, Heather supports her husband and teenage daughter and a menagerie of pets.

Tracy Hecht, Ph.D., is professor of management and graduate program director of the Ph.D. program in business administration at the John Molson School of Business, Concordia University in Montreal, Canada. She is also associate editor at the *Journal of Organizational Behavior*. Her research focuses on the work-nonwork interface, aiming to understand how interactions among work, family, and other life roles affect job search processes, careers, and well-being. Tracy teaches courses on human resource management, organizational behavior, and research methods at the doctoral, master's, and undergraduate levels. Her marriage of 20 years to a husband who is an equal partner in household labor and parenting has been one of the key ingredients in her successful career.

Brian Page spent 15 years as a personal finance and economics educator. He was recognized as a National Educator of the Year by the Milken Foundation and Ohio Department of Education, a CNN Money Hero, and a former Working Group Member of President Obama's Advisory Council on Financial Capability. Brian transitioned to a senior-level position with Next Gen Personal Finance when he moved to Atlanta to support his wife's career. He later served a one-year term as a Visiting Scholar at the Consumer Financial Protection Bureau in the Office of Youth Financial Education. Brian is the founder of Modern Husbands, which is dedicated to sharing ideas on managing money and the home as a team.

Eden Pontz is an award-winning journalist, media professional, and mother. She is executive producer and director of digital content at the Center for Parent and Teen Communication at Children's Hospital of Philadelphia. She was previously executive producer at CNN's New York/Northeast Bureau, overseeing domestic newsgathering for more than a decade. She has reported, blogged, and created videos, podcasts, and written content on a wide range of topics, including health, science, technology, and entertainment.

Andrew C. Pool, Ph.D., MSc, is a research scientist at the Center for Parent and Teen Communication at Children's Hospital of Philadelphia. He has a doctorate in public health with a concentration in social and behavioral sciences from Temple University and a master of science degree in evolutionary psychology from the University of Liverpool. He has worked in psychological and public health research for 15 years. His research interests include parenting, adolescent development, and effective translation and dissemination of scientific findings.

Jennifer Sabatini Fraone is executive director at the Boston College Center for Work & Family, where she oversees corporate relations and programming for the Boston College Workforce Roundtable, a premier learning and networking community for HR leaders at progressive organizations, and supervises the Center's primary and secondary research efforts. Jennifer collaborates with and advises global organizations on topics such as parenting and caregiving, workplace flexibility, inclusion and belonging, employee well-being, career development and management, and improving the total employee experience. Jennifer and her husband, John, are the proud parents of two young adults.

Susan Russo spent more than 15 years as a strategic HR leader for private and global *Fortune* 500 companies before starting a family and pivoting to independent consulting and academia. Now, she creates and delivers engaging leadership development programs for audiences of all sizes. Her work has been published by international professional publications and she regularly speaks at conferences and associations. She is an adjunct professor of strategic human resource management, organizational behavior and leadership, and ethical decision-making at the Fairleigh Dickinson University Silberman College of Business.

Alyssa F. Westring, Ph.D., is Vincent de Paul Professor and chair of the Department of Management and Entrepreneurship at the Driehaus College of Business, DePaul University. She is coauthor of *Parents Who Lead: The Leadership Approach You Need to Parent with Purpose, Fuel Your Career, and Create a Richer Life* with Stewart Friedman. An award-winning educator and Certified Diversity Professional, Alyssa shares her expertise on leadership, women's careers, and work-life integration in leading academic and popular outlets and is a frequent speaker at *Fortune* 500 companies.

Introduction

Scott Behson, Ph.D.

In my opinion, teenagers get a bad rap.

Teenagers are amazing! Sometimes, I wish we were all more like teenagers.

I have a teenager of my own, and watching him and his friends grow up taught me a lot about life. I've also had the privilege to work with college sophomores for the last 25 years, and they've taught me so much. My wife, among her many jobs, coaches young stage performers and directs youth theater, and she has learned from them, as well. Despite the drama and difficulties, I've come to the conclusion that teenagers are amazing.

My biggest piece of advice to parents of teenagers is to start from a place of empathy for what their teens experience.

Seeing things from their point of view can be hard because, often, we still see our children as "ours." When kids are little, they actually are mostly "ours." They are our world, and we are theirs. During early childhood, they only slowly and gently become part of a wider world—extended family, teachers, a handful of carefully curated friends, and a few select caregivers.

During the teenage years, however, this tightly constructed world is blown open, and our children are no longer just, or even primarily, ours. They are now part of a wider society, with many things affecting them, including issues like global warming, economic woes and their first jobs, and—especially—their peers, friends, frenemies, and others at school and in their social lives. Parenting a teen is a huge adjustment from parenting a younger child.

Teens live their lives very publicly and are brave enough to try new things all the time. Teenagers perform at piano recitals and school plays, play field hockey, and run track—voluntarily putting themselves in the spotlight even while they're developing new skills. They're succeeding, failing, and learning all under the watchful eye of their peers, parents, and, increasingly, the entire world through social media. When they fail, they get back up and do it again. They're so resilient.

Consider that, in high school, sometimes even the simple act of sitting at a new lunch table, taking a different class, wearing a different style, or "trying on" a new facet of your personality is done under the literal scrutinizing eyes of your peers. Teens' peer circle is also much wider than it used to be; social media represents another crowded, tempting, cliquey, global lunchroom full of cool teens showing off and dubious role models applying social pressure. In fact, the Pew Research Center found that both teens and parents believe that being a teenager today is harder than it was for prior generations because of the dark side of social media and technology, high pressures and expectations, and feelings that the world and country have changed for the worse.[1]

Teenagers may start out as "big kids" who are still largely defined by their families and small group of friends. They quickly transition to

---

[1] Michelle Faverio, Jeffrey Gottfried, Kaitlyn Radde, Chris Baronavski, and Sara Atske, "Why Many Parents and Teens Think It's Harder Being a Teen Today," Pew Research Center, August 27, 2024, https://www.pewresearch.org/internet/feature/why-many-parents-and-teens-think-its-harder-being-a-teen-today/

something entirely new and vastly more complex. They grow out of old friendships and into new ones. They have their first romantic relationships, which also involves bravery in trying new things (for good and bad). They're learning as they go, so, of course they make lots of mistakes, leading to drama, breakups, and heartbreak. They learn, bounce back, and engage in new relationships, once again proving their resilience.

Teenagers today are tempted by all the things that have always tempted teens, plus modern temptations, as well. They experiment (even when they shouldn't), and they learn. They succeed, and they fail. And they get up again.

Yes, teenagers can be moody, unpredictable, and impulsive. They make really dumb and thoughtless mistakes. They haven't learned to properly calibrate risk and danger. They are ever-changing. They desperately want to be grown up and they also want to stay kids a while longer.

Despite all the chaos they cause, I've long thought teenagers get an undeserved reputation from the rest of us.

In fact, University of Calgary historian Paul Fairie has collected reams of newspaper clippings and headlines from the past century or so, observing that certain assertions have been made seemingly forever. He posts his compilations on social media and is developing these lists into a book. His collection of articles on how "teens today" are too rowdy, soft, undisciplined, and rude includes almost-identical headlines and arguments from 1921 ("Kids have it too soft for their own good"), 1931, 1942 ("Modern school kids are too soft"), 1955, 1961 ("Are our children too soft to face the adult world?"), 1977, 1989, 1994 ("... kids today get driven to Little League! Kids are too soft, a bunch of marshmallows"), 2008, 2016 ("Are kids too soft today?"), and 2024. Same as it ever was.

I mean, can you guess who wrote this?

> "Our youth now love luxury. They have bad manners, contempt for authority; they show disrespect for their elders and love chatter in place of exercise; they no longer rise when elders enter the room; they contradict their parents, chatter before company; gobble up their food and tyrannize their teachers."

Socrates, in 420 B.C.!

Being a parent of a teenager is often emotionally fraught. We root for our kids so hard that we sometimes put pressure on them without even realizing it. Sometimes we grip too tightly or hover too close. We try to protect them. Sometimes we step aside to let them fail. Often, we get shoved out of the way and pushed temporarily to the margins of their lives (they have to learn to be independent, so this is natural, albeit crushing). We need to stay open-hearted, even when it hurts. Sometimes we simply need to ride out the storm. We constantly feel put on the wrong foot. The teenage years are new to us, too. The best we can do is try, succeed, fail, and get back up again. If we're lucky, we pick up on our teens' resilience.

In this book, and in other books from Parent Ready, experts and peers share practical advice backed by legitimate research to help you navigate these turbulent years and be the best support you can for your teenager while maintaining your sanity.

In this volume, there are chapters about issues teenagers often face. By extension, these are issues that you, as the parent of a teen, also need to face head on. We discuss how the teen years change family dynamics, budgets, and priorities. You'll learn some lessons and get great advice on how to navigate home life while adjusting to the pressures brought on by the teen years, brought to you by psychologists, family counselors, and other experts, most of whom are also navigating life while parenting teens.

This book also serves a second, very important purpose.

There are a lot of books on parenting, and there are lots of books on career advice. But it is very rare that parenting books also address career *concerns*. It's even rarer to find a career book that addresses the intersection of work and family. Considering how inescapably linked work and life are, I think this lack of integration represents a huge blind spot! As a result, most parenting books and career books are far less effective than they should be. (I'm proud that one of my previous books, *The Working Dad's Survival Guide: How to Succeed at Work and at Home* (2015) focuses on both, helping fathers navigate both career and parenthood.)

The fact is, on a given workday, most adults spend about eight hours at work, eight hours sleeping, and eight hours attending to family and other responsibilities. I think it's long past due that books relating to parenthood discuss how it intersects with managing careers.

I'm proud to say this book will fill the gap.

In addition to the emotional whirlwind of raising our teenagers, we parents also face a new set of time demands and work-family conflicts. Logistics, planning, time management, and financial planning become incredibly important.

Many teens are involved in multiple after-school activities. Getting them where they need to go as "Mom and Dad's taxi service" can sometimes feel like an all-consuming task. We need to juggle their schedules with those of our work, leading to sometimes impossible trade-offs and difficult choices. Plus, the pressures we face on the emotional side of parenting our temperamental, multidimensional teens can lead to distractions and interruptions that hold us back at work. We won't always get it right. We'll try, we'll fail—but hopefully we can emulate our teenagers and learn to be resilient.

When we had younger kids, our coworkers and managers loved to hear about them (or at least tolerated our cute toddler stories) and tended to be at least somewhat understanding when our kids' needs conflicted with work hours. Not so anymore. No one wants to hear about our teens' angst or acne, and it's awkward to share their struggles (no one has sympathy when a teen gets suspended for vaping in the locker room!). Coworkers, bosses, and work cultures are less supportive when work and parenting demands clash, but we still need the time and support to be present parents for our teens.

Further, at this point in our lives, most of us are midway or more into our careers and have significant work responsibilities. We care about doing a good job, providing for our families, and doing right by our customers, bosses, direct reports, and clients. So many rely on us. We're also thinking ahead to the finances that might be required for our children's college educations, our family's health care, and our own retirements (which are coming up sooner than we think).

Some of us are challenged by caring not only for our teens and younger children, but also for our elder parents or others who need us. Happily, many of us have good partners who share in the workload. Others face the challenges of solo parenting or co-parenting with an ex after a messy divorce. None of this is easy. Doing it all at work and home sometimes feels daunting and impossible.

To help you with your work and teen-parenting demands, this volume includes chapters written by business school professors who have long studied the intersection of work and family (and, incidentally, teach older teens/young adults as part of their jobs). Others are penned by human resources professionals who have helped scores of employees navigate their work-life challenges and by best-in-class organizational consultants who have helped managers and employers better support their employees.

They provide actionable advice on protecting family time from the creeping demands of work, as well as time management tips and ways to partner with your teen, co-parent, and others to make it all work. They offer guidance on constructing appropriate boundaries so that you can attend to work demands and advance in your career without neglecting things at home. They also discuss balancing being a parent to a teen with other caregiving responsibilities. Finally, they provide perspective on how workplaces and managers can be more supportive of employees facing work/teen challenges, how we can leverage these resources, and how we can support our coworkers and peers. All this to help you navigate the dual challenges of parenting teens and succeeding at work.

More than any one great piece of usable advice (and this book has tons!), I think the main lesson of *Work-Family Ready* is that, even though it might be hard at times, parenting a teenager while balancing work and family is not impossible. We can succeed in both roles. We can rise to our challenges. We will fail, succeed, and learn. We'll become increasingly resilient. Navigating these new challenges and emotionally uncertain waters will make us feel almost as if we were teenagers again.

And, if I haven't made it clear by now, that can be a good thing, as I think teenagers are amazing!

Part I

YOUR WORLD IS CHANGING

Chapter 1
HOW DOES HAVING A TEEN CHANGE YOU?

Andy Pool, Ph.D. and Eden Pontz

You are standing in line at the grocery store, and your 9-year-old squeezes your hand and smiles at you. They like spending time with you. As you wait, the person behind you interjects to say: "Enjoy that sweetness while you can. Pretty soon, they'll be a teen, and they'll be a nightmare."

Does this sound familiar? Parenting is a constantly evolving journey shaped by the developmental stages of our children. During adolescence, this journey takes on new complexity as children transition from dependence to autonomy. Adolescence lasts from approximately ages 10 to 25 and is marked by profound physical, cognitive, emotional, and social changes. These shifts inevitably impact family dynamics as parents adjust their roles to meet the changing needs of their growing children. Parents go from primary decision-makers to guides and mentors as their teens approach adulthood. It's an exciting and sometimes challenging time.

In this chapter, we will explore the changing role of parents as their children move through the preteen and teenage years. We'll examine key developmental milestones in adolescence, their influence on family relationships, and strategies for fostering a healthy, supportive environment during this transformative period. By understanding these strategies and the developmental changes your teen is going through, you can create a nurturing home and feel prepared for the journey ahead.

Understanding Adolescence: A Time of Transition

Adolescence is a bridge between childhood and adulthood, marked by rapid development across several domains.

Physical and Biological Changes

The onset of puberty heralds a cascade of physical transformations. Hormonal changes lead to growth spurts, the development of secondary sexual characteristics, shifts in energy levels, and—for many—a heightened awareness of body image. These changes can sometimes lead to self-consciousness, mood swings, increased sensitivity, and identity confusion, all of which require parents to adapt their communication and support strategies.

For example, imagine a mother who is unsure what to do when her previously confident teen stops going out socially after breaking out with bad acne. She knows she needs to talk with her daughter but doesn't want to hurt her feelings. So, she begins by recounting some of her own difficult teen experiences. After listening and sharing, they can move on to discuss how they can address both her physical and social concerns.

Cognitive Development

Adolescent brains undergo significant restructuring, particularly in the prefrontal cortex, which governs decision-making, impulse control, emotional regulation, and planning. This restructuring is accompanied by heightened emotional reactivity, often driven by the limbic system (our emotional nervous system). Adolescents become more capable of abstract thinking, problem-solving, and questioning authority as they seek to establish their own moral compass.

This newfound critical thinking can result in disagreements with parents and offer opportunities for richer, more meaningful conversations. One dad was frustrated that he was constantly arguing with his son about being on his smartphone. He was worried that his son was becoming addicted to the phone. He decided to keep an open mind and talk to his son about his concerns. He explained his worry that too much phone use might negatively impact his son's mental health. His son said that he often used his phone for homework assignments and communicating with friends. Together, they set up a time limit for daily phone usage. This limit allowed his son to use the phone for necessities, plus a little extra. His father said that he'd consider expanding the phone limit if his son demonstrated responsible phone use and made good arguments as to why he needed more time.

Social and Emotional Growth

Adolescents strive for independence and self-identity while remaining tethered to their families. Friendships and peer influence take on increased importance, often challenging parental authority. Simultaneously, adolescents explore romantic relationships and grapple with a growing awareness of societal expectations. This balance requires parents to be patient and empathetic in new ways. Imagine a mother who was happy her son made new friends but worried about what they were up to when he broke curfew one Saturday night. This should lead to an important talk with him about rules and consequences, while also validating the importance and excitement of making new friends.

The Evolving Role of Parents

As children enter adolescence, traditional caregiving roles and direct supervision give way to new opportunities, challenges, and responsibilities. Parents must now expand their role to accommodate teenagers' growing autonomy.

From Manager to Consultant

Parents often act as hands-on managers in early childhood, making decisions about their children's daily routines, education, and social activities. During adolescence, the parental role shifts toward being a consultant who offers guidance while encouraging independence. This transition requires parents to relinquish some control, trusting their children to make decisions and learn from their mistakes. For example, rather than dictating how a child should handle a problematic peer, a parent might discuss possible approaches and encourage the child to choose one. As one dad said to his fatherhood and parenting group: "When your kids are young, you are Batman. When they become teens, you have to embrace becoming Robin."

Balancing Autonomy and Boundaries

Adolescents crave independence but still need structure, support, and love from their parents. Parents must strike a delicate balance between granting autonomy and enforcing boundaries. Open communication and collaborative rule-setting can help establish mutual respect and trust.

We recommend a style called Lighthouse Parenting,[2] which means guiding teens through adolescence's choppy waters, ensuring they safely arrive at the shore. This approach is showcased by one couple we know who decided, because their son did so well academically during freshman year, they'd stay hands-off about checking up on his homework as long as he maintained his grades and showed good study habits during sophomore year. Happily, he rose to the occasion. In one class where he fell behind, they checked on him until he resolved the issue himself.

Emphasizing Emotional Support

Teens will test boundaries during adolescence, and this can strain parent-child relationships. The emotional turbulence of adolescence often demands heightened parental empathy. Parents who model emotional resilience—listening without judgment, validating emotions, and remaining calm—show skills critical to maintaining a strong parent-child connection. When one father we know learned that his son was upset and dealing with a breakup with his girlfriend of two years, he thought to himself, "He's only a sophomore. There will be plenty of other fish in the sea." But when he thought further, he realized that what his son needed instead was for him to simply listen and validate his hurt feelings.

Modeling Healthy Relationships

As adolescents navigate friendships and romantic relationships, parents play a crucial role in modeling healthy communication, conflict resolution, and respect. These lessons often influence how teens approach their interpersonal relationships. For example, if your kids see you and your spouse arguing, you can follow up with them the

---

2 This term was coined by Dr. Ken Ginsburg, an adolescent medicine specialist at Children's Hospital of Philadelphia and founding director and director of programs at the Center for Parent and Teen Communication.

next day to discuss how you resolved your argument, apologized to each other, and came to a compromise. Better yet, let them see you settle the argument constructively (see page 9 for an example).

Championing Identity Formation

Adolescents explore their identity through experimentation, whether in fashion, music, hobbies, or social causes. Parents must support this exploration while ensuring a safe and respectful environment. Effectively supporting teens' identity development means being open to changes in preferences, respecting individuality, and encouraging self-expression.

One teen grew out his hair, dyed it black, and dressed in a goth-metal style. When his mother was asked how she felt about this, she responded, "I mean, I don't like how it looks, but it's his hair, his choice, and he'll probably grow out of this phase. He's a great kid who's taking care of everything he has to do, so I'm not really concerned." In other words, like this mom, consider giving your teen wide latitude in choosing how they dress, decorate their room, and make choices in what they watch and listen to. Teens need the space to explore identity and express their individuality within bounds of reason, safety, and propriety.

Managing Sibling Relationships

Siblings are often constant companions during childhood, but adolescence can shift these relationships. Increased conflicts and demands for privacy are common, with teens seeking more independence and less time with siblings. You may hear things like, "Stay out of my room!", "Don't touch my things!", or "Leave me alone!" While this newfound friction can be emotional for the family, it also has positives. Disagreements offer practice in respectful communication, conflict resolution, and empathy. You may have to help siblings manage the transitions in their relationships, leading with listening and empathy for both sides. Encouraging mutual support and understanding helps strengthen their bond, even if they aren't always in sync. After all, siblings provide a constant sense of belonging and support, especially when friends aren't around.

Coordinating with Your Spouse or Partner

Your partnership with a spouse or co-parent can be the key to parenting success. You need to coordinate decision-making to prevent mixed messages—like when one parent gives a different answer from the other. Your teen is watching, so be sure to work in tandem, even when you disagree or struggle balancing your heavy schedules. You should be aligned on your parenting style while openly discussing your decisions, and, importantly, involving your teen in discussions of rules and responsibilities. For example, you and your spouse can debate (without yelling!) in front of your teen, using questions such as, "I'd like to hear more about why you felt okay letting him go to the game even when his weekend chores weren't done." These discussions can teach teens problem-solving and respect. You demonstrate effective co-parenting by modeling teamwork and helping your teen learn from your example (more on this topic is in Chapter 5).

The Role of Extended Family

Your extended family plays a crucial role during adolescence. Aunts, uncles, cousins, grandparents, and close friends provide trusted support when parents are busy. They offer emotional and practical help, act as role models, and reinforce values or cultural traditions, providing different perspectives from parents. Sometimes teens are more willing to accept guidance from people other than their parents—even if they receive the same advice they rejected from you last week! This additional support doesn't mean teens need you less; it broadens their positive influences. Extended family helps teens appreciate heritage, strengthens their sense of belonging, and teaches them to view situations from multiple angles.

The Importance of Friends and Peers

Friend and peer relationships are essential for teens. They offer an emotional rush due to the increased dopamine—a neurotransmitter that makes us feel good—circulating in the brain when around friends. Teens observe, learn, listen to advice, and navigate successes and failures with peers.

Instead of trying to control their friendships, communicate concerns calmly and suggest questions to guide their decision-making, especially around risky behavior. Encourage them to ask themselves, "Would my parents be okay with me doing this? Am I putting myself at physical risk? Will I feel embarrassed if something goes wrong?" Remember, friendships evolve, and it's normal for teens to have shifting social circles. Trust their ability to grow through these experiences. Further, be sure to meet and build relationships with your teen's core friend group. One idea is to be the host family for their get-togethers or movie nights. Also, try to connect with the parents of your teen's friends. They can be valuable resources (and become new friends for you!).

Practical Strategies for Parents

Here are some practical strategies, based on teen development research, to help you and your family during these sometimes-challenging times.

Foster Open Communication

Teens need open communication with important adults, especially during struggles. When we see our kids struggle, it's tempting to offer quick solutions, but teens mostly need you to listen instead. Avoid interrupting or reacting too quickly and assure them they can speak without fear of punishment. By being attentive, patient, and non-judgmental, you'll encourage your teen to talk openly and confide in you. Active listening creates a safe space for honest conversations. For busy parents, carving out regular moments for these interactions at times when emotions are calm—perhaps at family dinner or downtime before bed—helps maintain this crucial connection.

Set Boundaries with Flexibility

Think of adolescence like a jigsaw puzzle. Your teen is trying to answer many questions to discover who they are—these are the puzzle pieces. Parents can help by building the corners and edges of the puzzle through setting boundaries and discipline. These boundaries are vital for helping teens navigate risk and safety. Teens test limits and seek independence. Their questions—"You're such a control freak, why can't I…?"—reflect their efforts to push boundaries. You need to explain that rules are for safety, not control, and are put in place out of love and protection. Then work together to set flexible guidelines. When they show their ability to be responsible and trustworthy (for example, they consistently make it home before curfew), you can consider changing the guidelines (giving them a later curfew).

Celebrate Milestones

Dozens of developmental milestones take place during the teen years. From having a first romantic interest, making the honor roll, or earning their driver's license, it's a time of growth similar to babyhood—the changes may come at you quickly! You celebrated when your child first rolled over, crawled, or took a step. Adolescence is also full of moments to celebrate. Pay close attention as your child gives you glimpses into the adult they are becoming. Let them know you are proud when they show you their true selves, and celebrate accomplishments and strong efforts (e.g., being brave by trying out a new after-school activity or showing kindness to a friend).

Further, give your teen opportunities to take on more responsibilities and expand their skill set. Teens should be increasingly responsible for performing tasks like managing their schedules, doing their own laundry, packing lunch, or cooking dinner. Celebrate their efforts and successes, acknowledging that, while mistakes may happen (and you end up ordering pizza for dinner), these experiences are vital for developing resilience.

Encourage Healthy Risk-Taking

As teens test limits, parents should provide growth opportunities by surrounding them with positive influences and role models. You should encourage healthy risk-taking through positive activities like auditioning for plays, joining a debate team, or participating in sports, where they can learn from peers, failure, teamwork, and adult role models. Volunteering, after-school programs, and clubs help teens develop new skills, while household chores prepare them for living independently. These experiences protect teens from unhealthy risks by equipping them to navigate the world within safe boundaries.

Seek Support When Needed

Sometimes, parental support isn't enough to handle a teen's struggles, and professional help is necessary. Seeking help is an act of strength, not weakness. Whether you find support from extended family, school counselors, coaches, clergy, or doctors, reaching out shows how much you care about your teen and that you are willing to gather all the resources they need. Teens need to know they deserve to feel their best and get support from various sources.

• • • • •

The next time you find yourself in the grocery store line with your sometimes-surly adolescent, don't look back at the sunny child they used to be. Instead, look at the amazing teen they are, and look forward to the remarkable adult they'll become.

Chapter 2

HOW DOES HAVING A TEEN CHANGE YOUR HOUSEHOLD?

Brian Page, M.Ed., AFC®, Fair Play Facilitator®

Let me guess: You've hit the stage where your home feels more like Grand Central Station than a peaceful refuge. One kid's shouting they need a ride to soccer practice, another's asking for help on a last-minute science project, and the group text with your boss is blowing up at the worst possible time. Sound familiar? Welcome to the teenage years, where life is a whirlwind of schedules, hormones, and logistics. If you've ever caught yourself wondering how you're supposed to manage all this and still hold onto your sanity (and maybe your career), you're not alone.

The teenage years bring a unique set of challenges to work-family dynamics. As kids grow older, their needs shift—and so do the demands on parents. Decisions get more complex, schedules more chaotic, and stress levels can skyrocket. But with thoughtful planning, teamwork at home, and a little help from supportive employers, it's possible to create a work-family balance that works for everyone.

Here's the good news: You've come to the right place. This chapter isn't about perfect solutions (spoiler: there aren't any), but it is packed with real-world tips and strategies for surviving and thriving when work and family life collide in a house with teenagers. Ready to dig in?

Household Decisions: Parenting Teens Versus Younger Kids

When your kid was little, most decisions revolved around their immediate needs: meal schedules, bedtime routines, and choosing the right preschool. Now, with a teen in the house, decisions become less about survival and more about shaping their future. Think: navigating curfews, negotiating social media rules, deciding on college savings, and figuring out how much independence to give.

Balancing how much independence to give and how much control and structure to assert depends a lot on your teen and what they can handle. But deciding on issues like curfews (they'll always want to be as late as possible) or rules around social media (it's a part of their lives but too much of it is harmful) is a fraught, ever-changing balancing act.

These decisions can spark heated debates (hello, family drama), but they're also a chance to teach your teens critical thinking and responsibility. Involve them in the decision-making process whenever possible. Not only will it lighten your load, but it'll also help them grow into capable adults.

Checklist

- ☐ Hold weekly family meetings to discuss major decisions and the shared family calendar.
- ☐ Create a family contract for what you expect of your teen (e.g., chores, good grades, not getting in trouble, being

home by curfew) and what they can expect from you in return (e.g., allowance, paying for things, gradually increasing independence).

☐ Teach your teen to weigh pros and cons before making decisions involving time commitments and money. For example, before joining a third after-school activity, have your teen chart out what this would mean in terms of their free time, family time, or other commitments.

☐ Be consistent with rules, which is contingent upon you and your co-parent having each other's back no matter what. Once your teen finds a parent willing to break, it all falls apart.

The Budget: How Teens Impact Your Finances

Teens aren't cheap. It all adds up, from extracurricular activities to braces, new clothes, and the ever-expanding grocery bill. Then there's the big-ticket stuff like college savings, a first car, or a high school trip abroad. Balancing these costs while staying on track with your family's financial goals requires some serious planning.

An abundance of research shows that sharing financial challenges with teens can create problems for them. We shouldn't share major problems, but involving them in conversations and decision-making is often really helpful. If treated more like adults during these conversations, most teens will understand your family's financial limitations. A mindset of maturity with your kids helps you manage costs and sets teens up for future financial success.

Here's one idea that has worked for me. Rather than budgeting for back-to-school shopping, taking your teen to the mall, or ordering what they need on Amazon, empower them with the choices. Ask your teen for a list of required school supplies and other items they need for school or want for themselves. Provide them, in cash, with the amount of money you have budgeted for back-to-school shopping and tell them that they must purchase the school supplies, but all other spending decisions are left to them. Whatever they don't spend, they keep. Now your teen is incentivized to budget and save—saving money in the short-run and learning valuable skills for adulting.

Checklist

- ☐ Create a budget specifically for teen-related expenses. Use this opportunity to distinguish between high-priority items (e.g., travel soccer for the big teen athlete) and lower-priority items (upgrading to the latest iPhone when theirs is still working well) and to see where you can economize (many teens enjoy shopping at thrift stores).
- ☐ Set boundaries on spending for extracurriculars and other activities.
- ☐ Consider how you and other family members can budget and cut back. Do you really need all those streaming services? A teen who sees you economize is more likely to understand when they have to do so.
- ☐ Involve your teen in budgeting conversations to teach financial literacy, as shared in the example on page 17.
- ☐ Encourage your teen to contribute through the money they earn from part-time jobs or chores. For example, if they use the family car, ask that they pay for gas or pitch in for an oil change.

Scheduling Chaos: The Teen Years

If you thought your calendar was full when your kids were little, brace yourself. Teens bring a new level of complexity to scheduling. Between school, sports, part-time jobs, and social events, it's easy to feel like you're drowning in logistics.

Juggling multiple kids' activities can feel like running a small business. One has basketball practice across town, another has band rehearsal, and you're somehow supposed to be at both places at once. Sound familiar?

To keep your sanity, you and your spouse must focus on communication and delegation. Create a rotation system for responsibilities, and don't hesitate to lean on your community for support. Carpooling, activity swaps, and even just venting with other parents can make a huge difference.

I used to be a director for a large and very successful youth soccer club. Our highest level teams traveled the country for matches and tournaments. It was not uncommon for parents of exceptional athletes to have multiple talented children in the club. What I learned from these parents was the importance of advance planning to ensure they both spent time watching their kids. They often took turns with who they would watch when their kids were simultaneously in two different parts of the country.

Embrace the power of shared calendars and proactive communication. Digital tools can be a lifesaver here, helping everyone stay on the same page. Also remember that you don't have to say yes to everything. Sometimes, scaling back is the healthiest choice for everyone.

Checklist

- [ ] Use a shared family calendar (e.g., Google Calendar) so that everyone can see each other's schedule and update as needed. This may involve prioritization and choosing activities that minimize overlap.
- [ ] Schedule a weekly planning session to review everyone's commitments. Communicate openly and honestly with your teen about the limits of your availability, recognizing you sometimes can't do it all.
- [ ] Delegate where possible (e.g., carpooling with other families). You may find it helpful to use group chats with other parents to coordinate rides.
- [ ] Designate specific evenings as family nights with no outside commitments.

Transportation and Teens' Growing Independence

Teens and transportation are a double-edged sword. On one hand, if your teen isn't driving, you're likely acting as their chauffeur. Having a teen with a driver's license can lighten your load. One dad I know told me he got three nights a week back for himself once his son could drive himself to his gymnastics training sessions.

On the other hand, teen driving brings new worries (and insurance costs). That same dad confessed he worried about his son's driving at night and got stressed if he got home later than expected, fearing the worst.

For my family, public transportation is not an option. We are fortunate enough to be able to purchase a (very) used car for our kids and pay for the expenses, with one caveat: If they get into an accident or get a ticket, they are responsible for the increased insurance cost. We showed them how much it would be in advance. They understood the consequences. However, our motivation wasn't primarily financial. We believe our arrangement reduces the chances our kids will be careless drivers. After all, a parent's first priority is their children's safety.

Set clear rules around driving privileges and expectations, and work together to manage the logistics. Our decision regarding car insurance exemplifies an open, age-appropriate conversation about money with teens that reinforces driving privileges and safety expectations.

For younger teens, explore options like school buses, public transit, or rideshare apps (if age-appropriate).

Checklist

- ☐ Establish driving rules and boundaries (e.g., curfews, passenger limits) because teen driving is a privilege, not a right.
- ☐ Consider a shared family car for teen use, knowing that a shared car increases your need to set a family schedule.
- ☐ Enroll your teen in safe driving programs to receive insurance discounts.
- ☐ Create a transportation schedule that balances freedom and responsibilities. Teens who drive can run errands, too!
- ☐ As mentioned earlier, consider partnering with other families for carpooling or ridesharing.

Teamwork: Dual-Career Couples and Parenting Teens

For dual-career couples, managing the logistical needs of teens requires serious teamwork. Divide and conquer based on each parent's strengths and schedules. Remember, you're in this together.

The mental load—the invisible, cognitive, and emotional burden of managing household tasks—can significantly strain dual-career marriages if not equitably shared. Research has found that women shoulder more of the mental load of managing a home, which leads to problems in marriages. The division of labor in your home, which includes parenting teens, should be structured so that each partner has the same amount of leisure time and neither partner feels unfairly burdened by all the responsibilities at home.

Couples can create more balanced, supportive, and fulfilling relationships by acknowledging unseen work and employing structured strategies, such as clear delegation of responsibilities, a chore card deck system for dividing tasks,[3] or accountability checklists to better ensure equity.

Set aside time to discuss your priorities and strategies as a couple, and don't shy away from asking for help when you need it. Whether it's hiring a part-time sitter, relying on grandparents, building a network of other local parents, or leveraging workplace flexibility, teamwork extends beyond just the two of you.

For more on aligning with your co-parent, see Chapter 5.

Checklist

- ☐ Assign specific parenting tasks to each partner, making sure your division of labor is fair, considering work and other obligations.
- ☐ Check in regularly with each other about workload and stress levels. Ask for help when you need it.
- ☐ Seek outside help, including from friends, family, other parents, coaches, and tutors. Build a network that you can tap into.

---

3 Author Eve Rodsky wrote the book *Fair Play* to help couples tackle this issue and developed a set of cards that can be used to run a household more equitably. See her website: https://www.fairplaylife.com/the-cards.

How We Can Access Employer Support

Employers play a crucial role in helping parents navigate the teen years. Flexible work schedules, generous paid time off policies, paid parental leave, and supportive managers can make all the difference.

For example, managers—particularly male managers—can create a work culture that supports busy parents by parenting "out loud" themselves. Men can make a point of sharing with their teams when they need to leave work for doctor's appointments with their children or for other family commitments, helping break the gender norm of women always taking the lead in this area.

Employers can also creatively use hybrid work environments as an efficiency tool for busy parents. Why fight the traffic to work when that time can be used *for* work, while also allowing a parent to be home when their kid arrives from school at least a few days a week?

If your workplace lacks these supports, consider starting a conversation with human resources or your manager. Share ideas for parent-friendly policies, and don't be afraid to advocate for what you need. Chances are, you're not the only parent looking for solutions. See Chapter 12 for more about communicating with your manager.

Checklist

- ☐ Familiarize yourself with your company's parental benefits. There may be programs you and your manager are not aware of.
- ☐ Suggest parent-focused initiatives, such as family-friendly scheduling, work-from-home days, and ways for employees to swap shifts more easily.
- ☐ Take advantage of remote work and hybrid options when available.

- ☐ Be transparent with your employer, manager, and coworkers about your needs as a working parent. If they don't know your needs, they can't step up for you.

Closing Thoughts

Remember that chaotic scene we started with? The one where life felt completely out of control? Here's the thing: You're not alone in the madness. Parenting teens while balancing work is tough, but it's also rewarding. With the right mindset, strategies, and support systems, you can navigate this stage and come out stronger on the other side. And when all else fails, remember this: You're doing the best you can, and that's more than enough.

Chapter 3
HOW DOES HAVING A TEEN AFFECT YOUR WORK?

Karen Clark Salinas

Congratulations! You're now a working parent with a teen. Your years of parenting a teenager often coincide with what can be your time of greatest professional impact.

Consider approaching these years with curiosity about your *and* your teen's shifting identities. You've likely built significant professional expertise over the past decades. Now, as parenting becomes less hands-on, you may have more energy and time to invest in your career. Meanwhile, your teen is beginning to explore their professional interests. Your parallel journey creates opportunities for both of your career paths. Shifting family dynamics offer an ideal moment to reflect on how you show up as a leader—both at work and for your teen. This chapter will help you navigate both paths successfully so you and your teen can thrive.

Parents of teenagers face a set of career challenges that look very different from when their children were young. While managing young children meant juggling predictable schedules in environments you could control, the teen years bring a more complicated balancing act where you have less control, but the stakes feel bigger. The mental load shifts from handling daily physical needs to processing serious concerns about your teen's safety, emotional well-being, and future. Working parents frequently find themselves caught between career demands and the need to be present for meaningful conversations with their teen about relationships, identity, or life choices that can't be put off until later. This challenge gets trickier with teens' growing independence, which, surprisingly, requires more thoughtful and immediate parental involvement, even though you have less say in when and how that involvement happens.

Your Professional Foundation

What You Offer Work

As a mid-career professional, you likely have acquired some important skills:

- Expertise and perspective gained from years of working in your career
- Problem-solving, from navigating complex initiatives and challenges
- Ability to manage multiple stakeholders and competing priorities
- Facility with mentoring, coaching others, and aligning priorities

What You Need From Work

While you have increased freedom to respond to the demands of work as your child is more independent and can share responsibilities at home, you may sometimes need help from coworkers and leadership to help you rise to your work-family challenges. This help could take several forms:

- Schedule flexibility so you can deal with teen activities, events, and emergencies
- Trust that you know how and where you work best to achieve results
- Clear boundaries between work and home to allow you to boost energy, mental focus, and self-care
- Professional development opportunities that align with your evolving aspirations
- Financial well-being programs that can help you plan for and protect financial resources

Considering the above, the approaches listed in the rest of this chapter combine practical skills with strategic thinking to help you maximize your impact at work while parenting your teen and modeling valuable work-life skills.

Core Success Foundations

These fundamental strategies help you work smarter, not harder, which will help ensure that you have energy for both professional success and meaningful family time.

Managing Time and Energy

Understanding that energy—not just time—is a crucial resource revolutionizes how you approach your workday. While time remains finite, energy can be optimized through strategic management. As an example, when I managed a chronic illness, I needed to identify and leverage my peak cognitive windows, those golden hours when my brain operated at maximum capacity. I scheduled demanding tasks at the start of my workday, when my mental energy was highest, and reserved routine work, such as answering emails, for natural energy dips in the afternoon. I extended this approach to weekly energy patterns, realizing I could capitalize on post-weekend renewal by front-loading complex projects early in the week. As a result, I increased my performance and prevented burnout. These principles can help you achieve more by strategically focusing and timing the use of your available energy, both at work and at home.

Setting Boundaries

Setting boundaries isn't selfish; it's professional self-respect that enhances your ability to deliver results while giving coworkers permission to set healthy limits for themselves. Rather than walls that distance you from colleagues, boundaries are protective guidelines that teach others how to engage with you. This practice involves clearly communicating your needs, limits, and expectations, whether declining misaligned projects, protecting focused work time on your schedule, or establishing response time expectations in your email signature. For example, during my teens' soccer seasons, I adjusted my work schedule, communicating to my team that, on Tuesdays and Thursdays, I leave the office by 3:30 p.m. for games but will be available by phone for urgent matters and back online after 7 p.m. to handle any pressing work. See more on boundaries in Chapters 4 and 7.

Implementing the Triple Win

The "triple win" is a strategic framework developed by ThirdPath Institute[4]. This model helps us evaluate and navigate situations through three essential lenses: benefit to you, benefit to your work quality, and benefit to others you work with (these lenses can also be

---

[4] Author's note: I am one of ThirdPath's Integrated Life Advocates—learn more at www.ThirdPath.org. It's a national nonprofit helping parents apply the triple win at work and at home.

applied to home and family situations). Imagine you've been given the responsibility of leading an important work initiative, which leaves you both excited and overwhelmed, because you were already worried about current project deadlines. Using the triple win approach, you analyze the situation in three steps:

1. You need sustainable work hours to stay energized and to protect the time you need to be a present parent (good for you).

2. The new initiative could significantly impact quarterly goals (good for the work).

3. Delegating some current projects would create growth opportunities for team members (good for others).

This assessment leads you to accept the new initiative while redistributing some responsibilities, in consultation with your manager. This transforms a workplace challenge into an opportunity for collective success and your own well-being.

Applying the 80/20 Rule

Accepting you will always have more work than you can complete and that each task differs in its contributions to achieving business outcomes, the Pareto principle reveals that approximately 80% of one's results flow from 20% of efforts. Analyze your responsibilities through this lens to identify activities that generate disproportionate value.

I'm a big proponent of daily, weekly, monthly, and quarterly work-life planning to keep myself focused on things I must do (meetings and appointments) and things that create meaningful progress at work (e.g., an efficient staff meeting) or at home (e.g., family game night), while avoiding spending too much time or energy on less value-added tasks such as emails or laundry. In this way, I make choices to focus on the 20% of my daily and weekly responsibilities that provide 80% of the results. This approach, coupled with boundaries, energy management, and a triple-win mindset, should make you both more productive at work and a better parent to your teen.

Leadership and Influence

Apply your leadership expertise to set clear boundaries and accomplish more with less effort, creating positive ripple effects in both your professional and family life.

Delegating Effectively

Done well, delegation transforms both individual and team capacity. Start by identifying responsibilities you aren't uniquely qualified to do, then select team members based on their skills and growth potential. For example, in my coaching business, while I could handle the graphic design of my marketing materials, I recognized that my time was better spent serving my clients and crafting content that resonates with both current and potential clients' needs. By delegating the visual design to a skilled graphic designer, I freed up time to focus on serving my clients and growing my business. The designer not only executed the work efficiently, but they also brought fresh creative perspectives that enhanced the final product. This success came from clear communication about brand guidelines, a established review processes, and regular check-ins. This foundation of trust empowered both of us to do our best work (for more on delegation, see Chapter 7).

Seeking and Accepting Help

The ability to seek and gracefully receive support distinguishes mature leaders from those who insist on doing everything alone. We signal strength, not weakness, when we strategically ask for help. After all, no person is an island. We create opportunities for collaboration and mentorship when we identify where support is needed, determine whose expertise would be valuable, and frame our requests respectfully. As we develop the habit of asking ourselves, "What help do I need?", we become more aware of opportunities to support others based on our capacity. The reciprocity of seeking and accepting help contributes significantly to high-performing teams.

This principle extends to family life, where we must cultivate teamwork with our partners and teens, ensuring everyone contributes meaningfully. We model this by reaching out to other parents for support, recognizing them as additional sets of eyes and ears in our children's lives. These trusted adults become invaluable sounding boards when teens need someone to confide in about thoughts they may hesitate to share with us.

Sustainability and Well-Being

Build resilience through practices that balance high performance with intentional renewal, protecting your capacity to show up fully in all areas of life.

Practicing Recovery Cycles

High achievement in almost any career demands alternating between focused, high-intensity work and deliberate recovery to replenish your energy for the long term. During work "sprints," you engage fully in crucial deadlines or major initiatives, pouring in your time and energy to meet goals and deadlines (think tax season or a big client pitch). Similarly, you may face sprints in your family life when, for example, a loved one is ill or has an emergency. The key to long-term success lies in planning subsequent recovery periods, whether through technology-free weekends, dedicated family time, or a vacation. This rhythmic approach prevents burnout, while demonstrating healthy work-life integration to your coworkers and teen.

Cultivating Self-Compassion

Self-compassion offers an alternative to the perfectionism that often characterizes high-achieving environments. When you start to harshly judge yourself and your performance, shift your inner dialogue from criticism to understanding. After all, as a working parent of a teenager, you are handling so much while constantly attending to other people's needs. Remember that these negative thoughts aren't accurate depictions of who you truly are.

Instead of dwelling in negative self-talk, treat yourself with the same kindness you'd extend to a respected colleague, building resilience while demonstrating that excellence doesn't require harsh self-criticism. Be kind to yourself when you occasionally miss the mark. This practice becomes especially powerful when shared with your teen, as modeling self-compassion can profoundly shape their journey toward a more balanced and understanding relationship with themselves.

Communicating Intentionally

Strong relationships thrive on intentional communication that transforms everyday interactions into meaningful connections through observation, emotional awareness, and purposeful dialogue. Get curious and put yourself in others' shoes. Separate facts from interpretations, recognize that feelings stem from underlying needs, and create psychological safety for honest conversations. This approach strengthens professional relationships while modeling effective interpersonal skills.

You can also put intentional communication into practice when you notice your teen seems frustrated. Instead of immediately offering solutions, create space by saying, "You seem upset about something," and asking, "Would you like to talk about it?" By demonstrating this kind of attentive, nonjudgmental communication, you build an environment where deeper conversations flourish. Practice the same openness about your work commitments by explaining why they sometimes need to take priority, helping your teen understand how your work matters. Ask for their perspective, too. How do they feel when work takes precedence and what might help them feel more supported during busy times?

Managing Digital Boundaries

In our always-connected world, designing your digital boundaries serves both professional effectiveness and family connection. Use technology strategically. Set up Focus modes to filter notifications, for example. Keep work email or social media off your phone, and establish times when you're completely disconnected. Share your approach openly: Explain to coworkers why you don't respond to nonurgent messages after 8 p.m. and how you structure your remote work schedule to be present for after-school activities. Creating device-free routines—like a "no screen" rule during mealtimes or charging your phone overnight in a room other than your bedroom—demonstrates thoughtful technology management that prioritizes personal connection and well-being.

Growth and Connection

Transform career decisions into opportunities for deeper connection as you coach your teen through planning for their goals and dreams, while modeling how to integrate work and life as an adult.

Nurturing Parent-Teen Bonds During Career Transitions

Career transitions—whether you are seeking a promotion or considering a new role—create opportunities for meaningful conversations with your teen that strengthen mutual understanding, respect, and trust. When these conversations include your teen's aspirations, you should take on the role of coach rather than director, acknowledging their strengths and interests while offering perspective and guidance. When discussing your career moves, demonstrate trust in their judgment by asking for their insights. Share your thought process, showing respect for their growing autonomy, while teaching valuable decision-making skills that will serve them in their future transitions. These moments create feelings of pride as you see a more vivid vision of the adult your child is becoming.

Modeling Work-Life Integration

Children are always watching what their parents say and do. From early on, I treated school as my children's "job," using dinner conversations to draw parallels between their school experiences and my work life. I knew I was raising future professionals, so I deliberately showed them that career success means more than salary and title. Through my own choices, I demonstrated how to evaluate opportunities holistically, focusing on results rather than hours worked, balancing professional growth with personal satisfaction, and prioritizing family time and well-being. When considering career changes, I involved my teens in discussions, sharing my decision-making process openly. This practical modeling helps teens develop their own framework for making career decisions that honor both ambition and life priorities.

Embracing the Journey Together

The teen years represent a unique window of opportunity for both professional growth and strengthening family bonds. As your teenager develops their identity and explores future possibilities, your own career evolution can serve as a powerful teaching tool. The skills and strategies outlined in this chapter not only enhance your workplace effectiveness, but they also create meaningful moments for connection and learning with your teen.

Remember that this journey isn't about perfection; it's about progress and presence. Some days you'll execute these approaches flawlessly. Other days you'll learn from missteps. Both experiences offer valuable modeling opportunities for your teenager. By sharing your professional journey—the successes, challenges, and lessons learned—you demonstrate that careers are dynamic paths of continuous growth rather than fixed destinations.

Your teen parenting years coincide with what is often your most impactful professional chapter. The experience and wisdom you've gained, combined with your teen's growing independence, creates space for deeper career engagement, while building a stronger parent-teen relationship. Embrace this phase as an opportunity to grow together, knowing that how you navigate your professional life today helps shape how your teenager will approach their career journey tomorrow.

Part II

STRATEGIES FOR PARENTS TO MANAGE WORK-FAMILY FIT

Chapter 4
SETTING BOUNDARIES AT HOME TO ACCOMMODATE WORK

**Heather Cluley Bar-Or, Ph.D. and
Tracy D. Hecht, Ph.D.**

Like you, we are the parents of teens. Like you, we also have jobs and careers. If you are anything like us, you find it hard to do your best work while also parenting teens. There always seems to be more work to do than time to do it—both on the job and at home—and it can be tough to make sure that your teen gets the attention they need without interrupting important work demands ("Dad! What's for dinner?" "Mom! Someone shared my picture on social and it's NOT great.").

On the upside, your time has probably become decoupled from their time in many ways. Teens can find their way to the bus stop and can be left home alone for stretches of time. Their growing independence may mean that you get more frequent and longer uninterrupted stretches of focused work, especially as your teen can also contribute to the household through chores like cooking, cleaning, and—*gulp*—driving younger siblings. It may be easier for you to stay longer at the office or to work more productively from home.

On the downside, teens have more extracurricular activities and busier, more complicated social lives, so you may find yourself zigzagging all over town for their activities or waiting at home for them to bring the car back so you get to work on time. You may also be wondering how your teen is spending their time or, even worse, worry that their newfound freedom may lead them to spend their time in unwise ways. The teenage years will require you to adjust your boundaries to make sure you are meeting your work goals but also monitoring, caring for, and connecting with your teen.

In this chapter, we discuss what we have learned from boundary research, and from other parents, about managing boundaries at home to accommodate work. We also offer some ideas for how to do this while parenting a teen.

What Are Boundaries?

Boundaries are the borders that we place around the different roles we play and the different aspects of our lives to create some clarity between them. This may seem simple enough, but as boundary researchers, we've learned that boundaries are quite complex. That's because boundaries are not one thing. They exist in time and space and inside our minds. They are set by the cultures in which we live, the organizations where we work, the routines and habits of our families, and the expectations we have of ourselves. In our research, we've found that not all boundaries are created equal. Some are flexible and leaky, whereas others are rigid and impenetrable.

Time Management

First, let's discuss time management. The advantage of a strong boundary around work hours, like a traditional 9 to 5 or other clear work shift, is that it can facilitate focus, coordination within work teams, and service to customers. Conversely, many parents find that schedule flexibility helps them to accomplish work and attend to their family lives in a way that makes it easier to be successful at both. One dad told us that he tended to work a "split shift," going to the office in the morning, taking care of family responsibilities in the late afternoon, and then resuming work in the evening from home. This worked well for his work team because he was able to take on the meetings with clients in earlier time zones that other team members didn't want to take, and he was able to be there for his teen for homework help and rides to sports practice.

For those of us who have flexibility, boundaries are still important, and it can be helpful to put boundaries around chunks of time that are big enough so that we don't feel fragmented. Time chunks may depend on the type of work you do, but some research suggests that 90 minutes is the smallest useful amount of time to fully involve yourself in a thinking or creative task. Also, many people have times of the day when they are at their most focused and times when they have a predictable energy slump. If this resonates with you, consider using your own energy cycle to assign more demanding tasks to those chunks of time when your energy is at its peak.

Workspaces

Boundaries are about place, as well. The advantage of working at an office is that it creates a naturally strong boundary that is conducive to focusing on your manager's, coworkers', and clients' needs with few interruptions from family. By contrast, working at home can lead to more blurring because work and family are happening in the same place. However, there are ways to set boundaries at home to signal where work is done. If possible, work in a specific area and use physical barriers or visual cues to signal where you are working. That way, everyone can associate that space with your work. For instance, if you have a spare room or home office, put a note with your work hours on the door, and close it while working. If you have less available space to designate for work, you may have to get creative by using noise-cancelling headphones, temporary curtains, or other solutions. Make it clear where work is happening and make that space comfortable and conducive to working—whatever that means for the kind of work you do and given the limits on the space available.

You should have conversations with your teen and other family members about when, how, and under what circumstances they can reach you when you are at work. Depending on your circumstances and the constraints of your work, this can range from "emergencies only" to "texts but not calls" or specific "check-in times." Some families coordinate which parent can be reached at any given time so that each parent has protected time for uninterrupted work and kids know who to go to for help. For example, as professors, we both have certain days and times when we are teaching, and our teens know to call Dad if they need a ride, a meal, or homework help, and Dad knows that it's his turn to respond. (For more on boundaries and partnering with your spouse, see Chapters 5 and 7.)

Role Transitions

Some find it helpful to create clear transitions that help us mentally switch gears from work mode to family mode or vice versa. For example, those who work from a home office might close the door and then re-create a mini-commute by going out for a walk to commemorate the end of the workday. Those who work at the kitchen table may pack things up and put them away at the end of their shift. Some people dress in work clothes even when working from home and change clothes when work is done. On the other hand, one mother told us that she continued to wear her power suit when waiting at her teen's sports practice to signal that she was still in work mode, and she found it afforded her some privacy. All these actions send signals to others about what mode we are in.

• • • • •

Putting these ideas together, the key is to have boundaries around times and places that can be reserved for work so that you can do your work effectively. Once you've determined those boundaries, you can protect them by communicating your intentions and preferences to your boss and colleagues, as well as to your family. Here are three thought exercises that can help you consider how to create boundaries that provide a custom solution to your specific work and parenting challenges.

Thought Exercise #1: How Can You Communicate and Co-Create Boundaries with Your Teen?

Communication is the key to boundary management. Unfortunately, communicating with teens can be tough. They can be tight-lipped, cryptic, and defensive. You might tell them, "I have an important deadline tomorrow, and I need to get some work done tonight." Your teen may respond with an eye roll, with no indication whatsoever that you have spoken, or with a screaming tirade about how you love your work more than you love them. Despite your frustration, it's important to keep the conversation going.

The teen years are the perfect opportunity to communicate about boundaries because teens are developing their own boundaries and preferences. Maybe your affectionate child no longer wants hugs. Or they lock their doors when they are on a call or in the shower. You can leverage their newfound interest in boundary-setting to discuss its importance, and then work together to create boundaries and time schedules that work for everyone. By partnering with your teen, you show respect for their growing agency and sense of responsibility.

Involving teens in creating a family schedule can be especially helpful because, as they get older, information about school and extracurricular activities may be communicated to them directly and not to you. If you want to know when you can plan for a working dinner or an early-morning meeting, having your teen share their calendar with you can help you to know when it will be realistic to meet these work demands. Many families simply share events by posting their schedules on the fridge or through a shared calendar app. Your teen may know about other helpful technology.

Having said all that, teens are fickle and moody, so you must meet them where they are. That may mean making yourself available when they decide they need you. You may have planned an evening work session, but your teen decides that's when they need to talk. Resist the tendency to see your teen as interfering with work when that happens—after all, boundaries should be permeable when necessary. If you don't respond to them when they come to you, the moment may not return. This also goes for modes of communication. You can meet teens where they are by using the modes of communication they use (e.g., texting instead of calling).

Working with your teen to create boundaries can help calibrate expectations and decrease interruptions, but at the end of the day, they are still teens with big emotions and pressing needs. Therefore, consider scheduling your more focused work earlier in the day when teens are at school and scheduling smaller or lower-impact tasks for the hours right after school or in the evening, when work is more likely to be interrupted. Balancing teens and work requires flexibility and, at times, leakier boundaries.

Thought Exercise #2: Do I Continue to Parent in the Same Way?

As teens get older and more independent, you may be tempted to erect firmer boundaries around work and let your teen parent themself. But teens still require supervision (mostly in person, but sometimes through monitoring phone/social media use). Research shows that permissive parenting can lead to more risk-taking behavior. At the same time, overly controlling parenting can lead to mental illness for young people, which is already a risk as people enter adolescence.

This may mean finding ways to watch them from a distance, so that you notice signs of distress or poor decision-making, while also giving them the space they need to develop. The transitional parts of the day, like after school, may be good times to monitor your teen. One dad told us his teen tends to tell him things in the car or at bedtime that they wouldn't otherwise disclose. Identifying these transitional periods allows you to understand when to preserve certain times for parenting and when to reserve other times for concentrating on work.

Parents may also need to strengthen mental and emotional boundaries so that they are open to their teens but don't take on their teens' big emotions or react in kind to their strong emotional displays. Teens can explode over the smallest frustration or disappointment. While it may be tempting to tune them out, and thus avoid the outbursts, you would then risk missing important underlying concerns during an age in which brains, bodies, and hormones are developing, as is their path to identity and independence. While teen emotionality creates chaos and arguments, engaging while keeping your cool is often the best strategy. By doing so, we can be more effective parents. Further, maintaining your own emotional boundaries enables you to stay focused and engaged later while at work, without letting your teen's emotions (or the argument you had last night) negatively affect your productivity.

Thought Exercise #3: Am I Modeling Healthy Work-Life Balance?

Your teen may pretend to ignore you or even tell you they hate you (they don't!), but remember that they are watching and learning from you. They know whether you find your work meaningful and fulfilling. They see the way you prioritize different roles and tasks. The way you manage and communicate your boundaries sets the tone for how they will do so. Role modeling is the unsung hero of parenting. We worry so much about taking care of our kids, but one of the best ways to raise them to be good, healthy, contributing humans is to be those things ourselves.

Family dinners and leisure time are just as important in adolescence as they were when kids were little, except now, they say they don't want to participate. Your teen may be perfectly happy to leave you to your own devices (both figuratively and literally) as long as you leave them to theirs. But resist that temptation. It may take some creativity, but leaning into their interests can make doing things together more enticing. For example, you might want to play a favorite video game with them (they will probably find it amusing how bad you are), set up a joint playlist on Spotify where you expose each other to new music, or let them pick the restaurant for family dinner.

And remember to put your phone away while engaging with your teen. Research has shown that parental "phubbing" (phone snubbing) is associated with more depressive symptoms and more problematic phone use in teens, including more phubbing on their part. Giving teens your full attention when you are with them leads by example. Showing them how to block time for work and family can help them learn how to block time for their schoolwork, their own jobs, and their busy social lives, as well as how to manage their work-life boundaries as adults. If you're lucky, your teen may even block some time off to spend with you!

• • • • •

As working parents of teens, we are responsible both to our employers and to our families. These dual responsibilities require creative approaches to boundary management—in terms of time, place, and emotions. With good communication and partnership with your family, you can find ways to protect and make the best use of work time while ensuring enough time and emotional availability for parenting mercurial teenagers. We can also model boundary management and work-life balance so that our emerging adults gain these skills. Healthy, well-considered boundaries can make for successful careers and thriving families.

Chapter 5

ALIGNING WITH YOUR CO-PARENT FOR EFFECTIVE FAMILY MANAGEMENT

Alyssa Westring, Ph.D.

In March 2020, my children were 9 and 11 years old and my new parenting book was set to hit the bookshelves. Then, as we all know, the world changed overnight. The book tour was canceled as flights and events shut down due to the COVID virus. In a matter of days, life as a working parent with children changed dramatically. Making decisions about co-parenting and navigating this new reality became an even more essential skill, because the days of operating on autopilot were over.

In the five years since, life has mostly returned to its pre-pandemic pace and pattern. But now, I am the parent of teenagers, navigating a new world of parenting challenges alongside my husband. I continue to research, write, and speak about working parents, but with new insights from the world of raising teens.

In this chapter, I bring those insights to you. I will share evidence-based best practices for co-parenting teens from my decades of research, along with tips and tricks from the trenches. Parenting teens is a wild ride, with unexpected new joys and complex new challenges. But, if you have the tools to collaborate effectively with your co-parent in this journey, you will feel a little more present, purposeful, calm, and connected while you are in it—and so will your teens.

This chapter is more than a set of life hacks for managing the demands of raising teens. In fact, throughout my research with hundreds of working parents, I've found that looking to experts for these "hacks" is often a misguided endeavor. Instead, when you take the time for deeper self-reflection and more meaningful conversations, the best solutions for *your* life and *your* family will emerge on their own. You don't need an expert to tell you which calendar app to use. That part is easy once you know why you want a calendar app in the first place and how it will serve your family life.

So, let's dive into the real work. Through my research, I can confidently say that, although this work takes time (and requires a pause from busy schedules and to-do lists), it's worth it for you, your co-parent, and your kids.

•••••

There are three key skills that I cover in this chapter. These skills are derived from studies on what makes an effective leader and how those same skills can help you be more effective in all parts of your life, including parenthood. These insights are drawn from my work with my long time collaborator, Dr. Stewart Friedman, professor emeritus at the Wharton School, and my coauthor on the book I mentioned, *Parents Who Lead: The Leadership Approach You Need to Parent with Purpose, Fuel Your Career, and Create Richer Lives*. Our research flows from the premise that individuals can have greater work-life harmony by bringing leadership skills to all parts of their lives.

Stew and I have shown that these tools can help co-parents navigate complex challenges across all domains of their lives. In this chapter, we'll explore how you, your co-parent, and even your teen can develop these skills and apply them to more effectively collaborate in the process of leadership that is raising a family. These are the three fundamental skills:

1. Understanding your core values as individuals and as a family
2. Communicating proactively
3. Experimenting together

> Throughout this chapter, I use the term "co-parent" to refer to the person with whom you share primary parenting responsibilities. While your co-parent may be a cohabitating spouse, your co-parent could also be an ex-partner, a co-stepparent, or even a close family member or friend who is helping you raise your children. Some parents don't have a co-parent. Regardless of the size and shape of your family, I hope the skills I describe in this chapter will be valuable as you embrace your role as a leader in your family.

Skill 1: Understanding Your Core Values as Individuals and as a Family

Imagine you are the CEO of an organization. Every day, you are inundated with questions about how you will run your business, from finances, purchasing, human resources, marketing, and so on. When faced with complex questions, the best leaders make decisions based on a preestablished set of core values.

Similarly, when you and your co-parent face the countless decisions associated with raising a teen, understanding your shared values will help you make key decisions with more clarity and greater alignment. Research shows that when parents are clear about their core values, they are better able to make decisions.

There are several ways that you can arrive at your individual and shared values. In my experience, the simplest approach is for you and your family members to do a quick internet search for "list of core values," and then follow the steps below:

1. Each of you make a list of core values.

2. Ask each family member to select their top five core values from the list they made in step 1. (You need a concise list that you can remember, talk about, and act on. When you look at your list of values, you might be able to craft an argument for why you value every single word on that list, but any more than five and it's hard to keep track of them all.)

3. Share what each of your five core values means to you in a few words. For example, if you select the core value of "love," what does that mean to you? Love could mean "having someone who understands the 'real me'," or it could mean "nurturing and caring for another person."

4. Discuss and identify the set of core values that best reflects your shared family values, starting with your co-parent and then involving your teen in the conversation.

These values are intended to help you prioritize what's most important and simplify decision-making in your family. This exercise forces you to think about what is *most* important. By doing this work, you will be better prepared to make individual and family decisions aligned with those values.

From seemingly mundane questions (like who is going to drive your teen to soccer practice) to more complex and impactful issues (like how to respond to your teen's obsession with social media), being on the same page as your co-parent provides a common language and road map for reaching decisions that work for your family. It can also do the same for you and your teen. By involving them as partners in this discussion, you show them respect while helping them learn valuable life skills.

Skill 2: Communicating Proactively

Once you have done the work of identifying your shared values, the next step is to make them a part of proactive conversations with your co-parent and your children about how you will live your lives. Whether at work or at home, most of us are not that comfortable or familiar with talking about our values. However, by digging a bit deeper to talk about what you care about most, you open doors for more effective communication and problem resolution.

If you have ever had a recurring argument with your co-parent or teen over something that seems trivial, this is a fantastic opportunity to practice bringing your values into the conversation. Rather than talk about this issue in the heat of the moment, find a calm time to talk with your co-parent about how to approach this ongoing frustration. By taking a deeper dive into the values that underpin this debate with your co-parent, you will have a more meaningful and productive conversation, reach a more informed decision, and be able to communicate with your teen as a unified front.

Here's a seemingly small example:

> Let's say a frequent source of irritation is the recurring nightly debate about who should clean up after dinner. Your teen says

they are too busy, your partner has work to catch up on, and you resent always being the one left to the task. On the surface, this conflict is about who is cleaning up after dinner. However, when you bring your core values into the conversation, you can have a more impactful conversation about this nightly source of frustration and the deeper issues it may also reflect.

Perhaps your perspective emphasizes your core value of fairness in the division of family chores. Your partner's perspective might prioritize developing responsibility in your teens. And, not surprisingly, your teen's perspective may emphasize the values of independence and control. Most likely, the reason there is an ongoing debate about how to resolve this issue is that multiple values are at play at once. It may be challenging, but to the extent possible, assume that everyone is both well-intentioned and logical, just driven by different values. By uncovering and talking about underlying values, you will be better able to understand everyone's perspective and, hopefully, identify new solutions that prioritize shared values.

Whether your issue is a small one like who cleans the dishes, or something bigger like work-life boundaries, risky teen behavior, or financial matters, using these questions can help guide you, your co-parent, and perhaps even your teen through these questions:

1. What is the surface-level problem from the perspective of each of the individuals in the situation?

2. What are the underlying values that are driving the perspective of everyone in the situation?

3. How do our differing values result in different perspectives about the "right" way to resolve this issue?

4. How are our core family values reflected in the situation?

Skill 3: Experimenting Together

As much as raising teens is an exercise in self-awareness and communication, it is also an exercise in managing complex decisions with no clear "right" answer. To be sure, understanding your values and communicating proactively will prepare you to make better decisions as co-parents. Laying that solid foundation is essential, but the next step is testing out potential solutions for your family when there is no clear right answer.

As a family, you do not have endless resources. There are limits to your time, energy, and money. Of course, you are also dealing with external constraints like school calendars, unexpected illnesses, work travel schedules, and so much more. Given these limitations and constraints, how do you find a path forward that works for your family?

This is where the temptation to turn to experts for the perfect life hacks comes into play. Whether it is finding the right app to synchronize your busy schedules, the right parenting technique to calm teen angst, or the right approach to managing social media, there is no shortage of expert advice, and it is incredibly tempting to want the single "right" answer to whatever challenge you are facing.

Often the best you and your co-parent can do is make an educated guess about what might work well for your family given your core values—and then try it. In my work, we refer to this process as *experimentation*. Starting with your core values and considering the reality of your current lives, what experiment could you try to help you address a parenting challenge? Going back to the example of cleaning up after dinner: Given your priorities as a family and your current reality, what might you try as a new and creative approach to managing the dishes? Do you devise a rotation system, implement a rule that "the cook doesn't clean," or make it a teen chore that contributes to earned allowance? Any of these, or something else, might make sense as an experimental solution based on your specific family dynamics.

When effective leaders design and implement experiments, they gather data, evaluate the results, and iterate by trying something new if the initial solution doesn't work. As co-parents, your responsibility is to do the same. If an experiment is working well, keep doing it. If it's not quite working as you had hoped, you can pivot or try something entirely new. In fact, even if you find an experiment that is working extremely well, it may not work well forever. The benefit of experimenting like a leader is that instead of feeling like a failure because you did not find the "right" solution, you can approach the situation with curiosity, compassion, and a commitment to continuous innovation and growth.

• • • • •

In summary, there is no single "right" solution to the challenges we face as co-parents raising teens. However, by framing parenting challenges as *leadership* challenges, you can leverage the decades of research on what the best leaders do. By doing so, you and your co-parent will become more aligned on your core values, more proactive in your communication, and more committed to experimenting with new and creative ways to thrive, not just survive, this phase of your lives. You'll be more likely to find approaches that work for your family dynamics and, even more importantly, you'll be raising children who are more likely to build the leadership skills to do this for themselves.

Chapter 6
PARTNERING WITH YOUR TEEN

Kelly D. Chandler, Ph.D.

"Kelly, why haven't you done the dishes since you got home from school? I've had a stressful day at work, and I need your help around the house!"

Fast-forward about 30 years, and I catch myself saying the same thing to my teenage daughters as my mom said to me. Apparently, there's a family legacy of aversion to doing dishes!

At the crux of the issue, though, is that both parents and teenagers are busy with many things in their lives that are competing for time, energy, and attention, including household chores.

Partnering with your teen to manage household tasks (especially dreaded tasks like doing the dishes!) can be mutually beneficial. Your teen will learn about managing responsibilities and develop life skills, and you can build a more mature relationship with your teen, while also creating more time for your career or other activities.

Both parents and teens experience the negative repercussions of role conflict. Work-family conflict is a significant stressor for American working parents, especially for mothers, who continue to do more household management, on average, than fathers.

Although it is often overlooked, teens, like their parents, experience conflict while managing multiple roles. Considering school, after-school activities, high-commitment athletics, school plays, time with friends, part-time work, college applications, and family responsibilities, one mother I know says, "There's probably no one busier than teens." Further, many teens have to work to help their family pay bills or provide care for younger siblings, which limits their opportunities outside school and for self-care. Partnering with your teen to thoughtfully and appropriately divide household tasks could reduce every family member's role conflict and improve family functioning.

Additionally, partnering with your teen to engage in household tasks can benefit them developmentally. Adolescence is a critical period for developing autonomy and individual responsibility and for preparing for adult roles. Many teens anticipate experiencing work-family conflict in their future. They can develop strategies in their teens that will enable them to manage their future households. Also, in families with allowance systems, teens can learn financial responsibility through household chores. Finally, it fosters family cohesion when teens recognize the joint responsibility of each family member to maintain the household.

Given these benefits, how can parents get reluctant teens involved in managing household tasks? In this chapter, I provide four evidence-based recommendations.

#1: Establish Expectations for Shared Responsibility in the Home

The foundation for shared household responsibility is the establishment of collective expectations. This foundation is built on clear and empathetic communication that results in mutual understanding. When you invite your teens to cocreate expectations about family responsibilities, you foster their confidence by demonstrating that their perspective matters; respecting their input can increase their buy-in to newfound responsibilities.

Cocreating these expectations starts with conversations about what constitutes a fair and just distribution of household labor. Should there be an equal division of labor among all family members? This may or may not be fair, given varying role demands in the family. Ideally, the division of labor should be equitable, with chores assigned that are proportional to an individual's capabilities, needs, and other responsibilities. To ensure a fair (and not necessarily equal) distribution, you'll need to consider various factors related to chores, the family, life circumstances, and individual family members.

The Division of Household Tasks

First, there are many factors about household chores to discuss with your teen: the types, quantity, frequency, timing, duration, and number of people needed to complete the work. The following questions may help you discuss chores with your teen:

1. How should the family prioritize and divide common household maintenance tasks, including meal preparation, dishes, laundry, trash, pet care, cleaning various rooms in the house, and lawn upkeep? How long does each chore take?

2. In addition to maintenance tasks, is there family care work for siblings or grandparents? For example, is a teen asked to drive younger siblings to sports or other activities?

3. What is the frequency with which these chores need to be performed—daily (e.g., pet care), weekly (e.g., cleaning bedrooms), monthly (e.g., a thorough house cleaning), or seasonally (e.g., clearing the gutters)?

4. For daily tasks, are there specific times that chores need to be done? With weekly chores, are these saved for weekends?

5. How many family members are required to complete each chore, and would it make sense to do them together? There might be creative ways to make the most mundane tasks more enjoyable if done together. For example, meal preparation can be a fun family activity.

The fit between chores and individual characteristics, including age, ability, health, interests, and personality, need to be considered to create a fair and just distribution of tasks. Living with a chronic health condition may limit what a teen can be expected to physically accomplish, for example. One teen may love the outdoors and volunteer to be responsible for lawn care, and another teen may jump at the chance to care for the beloved family pet.

Having an open discussion about each family member's abilities and interests to complete certain chores—rather than simply assigning tasks—should foster more satisfaction and engagement in the division of labor. In addition to abilities and interests, expectations should be contingent upon individuals' demands and resources (e.g., time, energy) across multiple responsibilities, such as school, paid work, after-school activities, and volunteering.

Family Composition and Functioning

Second, there needs to be a mutual understanding of how a family's composition and functioning influences how chores are prioritized and shared. Family composition (e.g., the number, ages, and roles of family members) provides a useful framework to start. This also includes the number of employed workers in the home, both parents and teens. For instance, it may be appropriate to load up a teen without a part-time job with chores, through which they can earn allowance, while easing off on teens who have part-time jobs. Further, the primary income earner often devotes more time to paid work outside the home and could be responsible for fewer daily household tasks.

Co-residence is an important factor, too. Depending on custody arrangements and parenting plans, children may alternate between two households with different expectations about shared responsibility. Teens with a single parent may need to shoulder more housework and sibling care compared to teens with two parents. There may also be additional housework if a grandparent or aging adult relative lives with the family.

Beyond family composition, family functioning shapes household responsibilities. Family communication, emotional climate, routines, relationship quality, parenting style, and other aspects are related to how well it can meet the needs of its members. For example, an authoritative parenting style involves setting clear expectations about chores, while also listening and being supportive and compromising when a teen is struggling to meet these expectations. Further, a teen desiring more independence can be given more autonomy in selecting chores and how they get done, while a teen experiencing anxiety may require a regular routine and clear directions. Establishing shared expectations is more complicated than simply creating a chore list.

Changing Circumstances

Third, changes in life circumstances require families to adapt their strategies to complete different tasks, including maintenance tasks. For example, a mom who works as a tax accountant may be less available to contribute to household maintenance during the busy tax season. Perhaps a teen or a partner can temporarily step up to do more of the cooking and cleaning. During basketball season, a teen may have to stay after school past dinnertime for practice and even later for games. Perhaps some chores can be deferred temporarily until after the season. While not all circumstances are predictable, the family can discuss expectations around how it will recalibrate responsibilities. After all, flexibility is an important characteristic of effective family functioning.

• • • • •

There are many factors to consider when cocreating a fair and just household management plan. Communicating the rationale behind decisions is crucial. Teens may initially feel put upon when they compare their workload to their younger sibling's. However, with good communication, they are more likely to understand the situation is related to capabilities. For example, maybe their sibling is too young to safely operate the lawn mower.

Of course, there may be no "perfect" solution, wherein everyone is satisfied with their assignments; thus, conflict is inevitable, and compromise is necessary. Finally, dissatisfaction and conflict can arise when there is a mismatch between expectations and reality. Therefore, there should be accountability for those who do not fulfill their responsibilities and recognition for those who do.

#2: Exhibit Positive Role-Modeling Behaviors

Parents who hold themselves accountable for their shared responsibility in the home are also serving as positive role models for their teens. Role modeling may be especially important for fathers who can demonstrate through their actions that household chores—even those more closely defined as "women's work"—are for everyone. For example, one dad I know made sure his kids regularly saw him cooking, cleaning, and doing laundry in an equal partnership with his wife so they would grow up with a less gendered view of household responsibility.

More generally, though, role modeling teaches teens about the value of shared responsibility in the home, to keep the household operating smoothly, to care for family members, and to create a positive emotional climate through teamwork. Parents can serve as positive role models by the way they manage their own conflict between paid and unpaid labor. For example, a parent may need to stay late at work, so they are unable to start making dinner on time. This parent could ask their teen to do the food prep or even prepare the meal. In return, the parent offers to (*gasp!*) take care of the dishes the next few days. This example demonstrates flexibility in managing multiple roles and the importance of teamwork to keep the household running smoothly.

As teens anticipate that they will face work-family conflict in their adult lives, watching how their parents negotiate competing role demands (perhaps through boundary-setting, delegation, and time management—see Chapters 4 and 5) could provide insight into strategies that are more or less effective.

Parents can also learn new perspectives and strategies from their teens. After all, teens juggle school, life, and family and can show us a thing or two. Finally, parents should complement their role-modeling behaviors by openly and honestly discussing with their teens how they negotiate work-life challenges, while inviting their teen's perspective and input.

Promoting Cultural Values and Priorities

Culture—values, beliefs, norms, and behaviors—is woven into household maintenance and can have a profound impact on families' daily lives. For example, some cultures may prioritize individual responsibility (care for oneself) over collective responsibility (care for the welfare of others), prioritize the honoring and care of older family members, or encourage traditional or egalitarian gender norms.

Parents who wish to promote their preferred model of division of labor in the household should ensure that their actions align with their words.[5] For example, parents may express the fact that they do not believe there should be gender-specific chores, yet, in practice, the mother often tends to do most of the laundry and the father does most of the car maintenance. Teens and parents can and should reflect on the extent to which their culture manifests in their household division of labor. While cultural values and household labor are complex topics, the key point is that families need to have a common understanding of the significance and meaning of the division of labor in their home.

#3: Empower Teens

Empowering teens to actively participate in how their household runs helps to foster their sense of self and belonging. The meaning of "home" is in part connected to perceptions about their rights to make decisions about how the household operates, including the division of labor. Inviting teens to the table—literally and metaphorically—to make joint decisions about household maintenance demonstrates that they are a valued member of the family. Having a voice is central to empowerment; parents can empower teens by creating a space for

---

[5] Editor's note: Priorities can also be communicated in the amount and types of chores assigned to teen boys and girls. I was raised by a traditional Italian American mom and had *no idea* how to do laundry when I went away to college. In contrast, my wife and I made sure our son did his own laundry and other chores starting in middle school.

them to advocate for themselves. Parents are often surprised at how well teens rise to the occasion when they are given the opportunity to do so.

Also, parents can foster teens' development of agency—the ability to make intentional decisions—in the context of household management. Partnership could involve creating space for teens to take on the responsibility for decisions about when and how they will complete chores, within reasonable parameters, recognizing that often there is more than one "right" way to do something. Partnership also means that parents should refrain from dictating the right way to do a chore ("the right way" often actually means the way you prefer to do it yourself). For example, after showing a teen how to load a dishwasher, you should step back and let them find their own method to complete their new daily chore, suppressing the urge to correct how they align the salad bowls. Unnecessary micromanaging or dismissing their ideas without contemplation interferes with agency and empowerment. In fact, one family I know uses the motto: "You can ask me to do something or tell me how to do it, but you can't do both."

#4: Express Empathy and Use Teamwork to Reduce Role Conflicts

Finally, an essential component of partnering with your teen is managing the family's emotional climate. Teens have busy and stressful lives. When teens are experiencing conflict among school, work, family, and other roles, parents can validate and empathize with their teens' feelings of overwhelm, perhaps by sharing ways they have successfully and unsuccessfully coped with role conflict. Parents can partner with their teen to seek ways to reduce stress, while still accomplishing household tasks. These moments provide opportunities for parents to demonstrate that the family is a team and can adapt when a member is having a difficult time meeting expectations. Teamwork reduces the impact of role conflicts and fosters cohesion, solidifying the parent-teen partnership while the parent models empathy and problem-solving.

Closing Advice

Both parents and teens have busy lives. Partnering with your teen to help maintain the household can benefit your teen and your entire family. These are four ways to build a strong partnership with your teen:

1. Establish expectations for shared responsibility in the home.
2. Exhibit positive role-modeling behaviors.
3. Empower your teens.
4. Express empathy and use teamwork to reduce role conflicts.

By following these recommendations, maybe your household will have more luck than mine in making sure someone gets the dishes done!

Chapter 7
SETTING BOUNDARIES AT WORK TO ACCOMMODATE YOUR FAMILY

Susan Russo

I recently observed this troubling scene at my local gym. As I was about to start my cardio work, I saw a stressed woman spend the better part of an hour standing next to the treadmill she was about to use, embroiled in her cell phone, on a call that could only have come from work. It was impossible not to overhear her side of the conversation, and it was clear that this was not a true emergency. I finished my workout before she could hang up and begin hers.

We all want to be the person who eats well, goes to the gym, and generously sacrifices our time for the benefit of others. As a working parent, carving out time just for us is simultaneously a luxury and a challenge. Imagine overcoming the hurdles of a bursting to-do list and competing demands from work and home and finally making it to the gym for a Tuesday morning workout, only to have it gobbled up by an urgent, but probably not emergency, call from work.

There is something about work that so easily bleeds into the rest of our lives. Often, we willingly let it happen, as if taking on extra tasks during our family time somehow makes us better workers or even better leaders. These work-related intrusions often have detrimental effects on our personal lives, physical health, and, often, mental health, but we still let them in. The negative effects become even more pronounced when we are raising families, especially for those in the sandwich generation who are raising families while caring for parents. Well thought-out plans and agendas often devolve into chaos, stress, and burnout. We pay a personal price, and our families foot the bill, too.

We allow this to happen because we often equate our work with survival. Our anxiety becomes magnified when we are working to ensure the livelihood of our children, particularly when they reach the age of being able to express their needs and wants.

Studies show that the same areas of our brain become activated during an emotional threat as with a physical threat. Work emergencies are processed in our brains the same way we process threats from a predator or other physical danger. The executive functions of our brain, which are the areas that enable us to be creative thinkers, effective strategists, and impactful communicators, are the very functions that get shut down when our amygdala is hijacked.[6]

Anyone raising a teenager is aware that strategy and communication are the pillars of success at home. But when a perceived threat from work arises, our amygdala shuts down these vital functions. On average, it takes 24 hours to recover from an amygdala hijack. So, that results in a full 24 hours where our reptilian brain is in charge of our thinking, decision-making, and communication.

---

6 An amygdala hijack is an emotional response that is immediate, overwhelming, and out of measure with the actual stimulus because it has triggered a much more significant emotional threat. The term was coined by Daniel Goleman in his 1996 book, *Emotional Intelligence: Why It Can Matter More Than IQ*.

It is critical for our health, safety, and relationships at home to put boundaries in place to protect our physical and mental space from workplace intrusions.

Workplace Roles

Employer expectations vary from role to role. Some roles are non-exempt, hourly jobs that receive overtime pay for more than full-time hours. In general, employers are mindful of not requesting extra hours at work unless there is a true work-related emergency or staffing shortage. Many workers in such roles willingly accept overtime work because of the financial boost it brings their paychecks. The benefit of extra work in these roles is obvious, and it is easier to delineate a boundary between work and home because legislation is in place to protect these employees from being overworked.

Workers in these roles should be deliberate in determining their must-haves for family time. Whether it's attendance at practices, games, recitals, or dinner, it is easier to enforce a boundary by determining what your must-haves are ahead of time. Set your schedule, block the time, and honor your boundary. Presence has an enormous return on investment.

Other jobs require on-call availability, and it is well-known in advance that we may be called away on short notice to work or support our organization. Parents who work on-call roles are typically able to fully disengage from work when they are not on call. It is as vital for our well-being to fully disengage during off-duty hours as it is to fulfill our duties when we are at work. Staying on call while we are off duty is unnecessary. When we fail to observe our on-call/off-duty schedules, our families pay a price. Be mindful of this if you often fall into the trap of failing to disconnect.

Most roles do not require scheduled on-call duty, but work-life blending becomes an inherent expectation of exempt, salaried positions. On the bright side, blending comes with the advantage of being able to step away between the traditional 9 to 5 working hours. Parents can attend school functions during the day and make it to games and practices that they might have otherwise missed. Transporting teenagers from place to place can become more convenient because of work-life blending. Overall, there are many benefits that did not exist prior to the adoption of technologies that allow for increased flexibility in where and when work can be completed.

However, work-life blending can quickly become bleeding if not properly managed. The onus is on us to protect our time and families from unwelcome work-related intrusions. There are several key steps we can take to set boundaries at work to accommodate our families that simultaneously enhance performance for our work teams and elevate our reputations as competent leaders:

1. Delegate effectively.
2. Define what is and is not an emergency.
3. Communicate your UN-availability.
4. Pay yourself first.

These steps are not only beneficial for our families, but they are also valuable for our employers.

Effective Delegation

Delegation is something that many people struggle with for a variety of reasons. Our fears range from imagining a problem that becomes a disaster unless we personally intervene to save the day to worrying about being replaced by someone else who was in the right place at the right time. In most cases, our fears are not reality. When we truly understand and appreciate the benefits of delegation, we become better leaders and better parents.

To delegate well, there are several actions to take:

- Identify the right person to take on a new responsibility.
- Provide them with the tools, information, and training to accomplish this work. This may take up some time in the short run but will save lots of time long-term.
- Provide clear boundaries and expectations.
- Inform others of your designee so that person will be contacted instead of you.
- Most importantly, trust your designee to rise to the occasion.

Delegation is a two-for-one special. By empowering others to take the lead on important matters in our absence, we can protect time with our families, while giving people the opportunity to develop their skill sets at work. This enables them to grow in their careers, and these meaningful opportunities increase engagement and retention at work. Further, most of us know that working for a boss who joins every call, shares an opinion on every topic at every meeting, and never disconnects from work is uncomfortable and demotivating. These behaviors demonstrate micromanagement, and no one likes to be micromanaged. We can both help ourselves and avoid demoralizing those around us by delegating.

Very few emergencies will pop up that truly require your immediate involvement, so give yourself permission to enjoy your time away from work by delegating authority to a trusted direct report or colleague. This will benefit you, your family, team, and organization.

Defining an "Emergency"

You may be wondering, "But what if an emergency does come up?" Not everything is an emergency, but all too often, we consider any question or message to warrant the same attention as a true emergency. This is why it is so important to define what "emergency" means ahead of time, and use this label sparingly.

What defines an emergency varies depending on the role you fill. In general, an emergency at work would be something that impacts the safety of people or the continuity of your business. Think about the types of situations that truly warrant your involvement. Discuss this with your team and agree on a definition. Your designee should know what you deem to be a true emergency that warrants an interruption from your family. Have an open dialogue with your team about what they would view as an emergency. Vet any assumptions about what you all believe warrants an interruption. Be proactive about letting people know what they are empowered to resolve in your absence, as well as what requires your involvement. Proactive dialogue is much more effective than reactive confusion.

Having these conversations is not only a preventive measure for protecting your time away from work, but it is also an excellent team-building activity. These conversations build connections among team members, which contributes to more cohesiveness and stronger relationships.

Communicating Your UN-Availability

Don't be afraid to communicate when you are truly unavailable. It may feel that the ubiquity of cellphones makes it impossible to be truly disconnected. But it is vital for our well-being to set boundaries at work to accommodate family. When a major life event such as a graduation or college tour is coming up, it is acceptable to request time away from work, and your employer should honor that request, especially if you have proactively delegated. But your employer can't do that if they don't know something important is coming up. To prevent a random call or text to ask if you "have a minute," let people know you will not be available. Your out-of-office email message should include contact information for your designee. We should be working to live, not living to work.

Pay Yourself First

In our roles as workers and parents, we become experts at putting everyone else first. Putting ourselves last is unhealthy and unsustainable. A great best practice for honoring the boundary between work and home is to define our absolute must-haves at home.

What are three things you absolutely must do each day? Whether it's related to exercise, diet, or personal development, start your day by accomplishing one of these items. For morning people, it might be ideal to start the day by exercising or meditating. For night people, it may be reading or journaling before bed.

Some of your must-haves probably involve your family. Carving out quality time with teenagers each day is not easy. Keep it simple so it's achievable. If sports or activities restrict the ability to share a family dinner, use the time in the car for a quality conversation rather than more screen time. Your teen can talk to their friends when they get to the field. Instead of taking a work call or logging into a Zoom meeting, you can use the ride to connect in a meaningful way with your teenager.

If you often play the role of teen chauffeur, consider putting together a playlist of favorite songs, alternating choices between you and your teen. This will likely lead to some great conversations and possibly even a shared interest in discovering new musicians.

If you aren't the one giving the ride, create and be consistent with a quick good-night ritual. Share thoughts with each other about successes from the day or even things you wish you could do over. Make it a point to share something you are each grateful for, too. Whether it's in person or from a distance, make the time to say or send a good-night message to your teenager at the end of each day. Teens may not admit it, but they need consistent connection to you.

• • • • •

Remember the woman I told you about at the gym? While the matter may have been urgent in that it took away her immediate attention, it did not sound like an actual work emergency. It didn't require her on-site presence. She didn't leave the gym. She didn't even leave her treadmill.

Imagine how this scene would have played out if this woman had delegated, defined "emergency," declared herself temporarily unavailable, and paid herself first. Her time on the treadmill would have reduced her stress instead of the interruption adding to it. The outcome would likely have been a well-balanced parent and worker ready to contribute productively at work and meaningfully at home.

Part III

CARE FOR SELF AND OTHERS

Chapter 8
THE PANINI GENERATION
Balancing Parenting Teens and Other Caregiving Responsibilities

Julia Beck

In theory, you should be thrilled. Your children are aging into their teen selves. It is a big leap for all of you because you have successfully loved and nurtured your babies into their teen years.

But your teen's ongoing development is not the only transition you are facing. While you have reinvented your parenting to match their growth, there are also other claims on your attention. You have evolved, your parents have aged, and your life has filled with responsibilities that are singularly yours and impossible to avoid.

Welcome to the Panini Generation

I've coined this term and prefer it to the oft-used "sandwich generation," because what we face includes far more heat and pressure being applied from all sides—kind of like we're being squeezed by a panini press!

Here are some simple facts about what our generation faces:

Fact 1: As your children grow, they require a radically different focus. In many ways, parenting teenagers becomes more difficult, as you are no longer the expert. Rather, you are a fellow newcomer navigating uncharted territory.

Fact 2: The average age of parents has risen over the past few decades due to factors like delayed marriage, longer periods of education, financial concerns facing young couples, and the time needed for career development. More people, probably including you, had your kids a bit later in life, which means you are likely in your late-40s/early-50s while parenting teens. You are likely facing an additional set of life demands than earlier generations of parents of teens faced. Namely:

Fact 3: The population of the United States is rapidly aging, with 10,000 people turning 65 each day. At this point in your life, you may have two parents, four with in-laws, and perhaps as many as six or even eight older adults in your life. These parents are now looking to you (or, unfortunately, denying they need anyone) for support. As they age, parents require more of your attention, be it for their health, finances, or a tangle of "all the things." Caring for aging parents can be a pressing and messy reality. Add to this the fact that extended families are less likely to live near each other than they used to be, which increases the logistical burden you face when trying to care for older relatives.

And your career? Your friendships? Your relationship with your co-parent? Your mental health? All of what you have lovingly cultivated is suddenly neglected in the name of caring for two generations at once.

Our culture has long demanded self-abnegation from mothers. Oprah Winfrey once asked Malcolm Gladwell[7] to describe the most selfless

---

[7] *Super Soul Sunday*, September 15, 2019, https://www.oprah.com/own-super-soul-sunday/malcolm-gladwell.

act he had ever witnessed. He answered: "Mothering." Ms. Winfrey agreed. They both described the long, thankless work of parenting, of women navigating the cycle of bleary-eyed days after sleepless nights and long workdays that led back to sleep-disrupted nights.

Caring for an aging parent takes a toll in a different, more challenging way. Thankfully, children become ever more capable, grow up, and move into their independent lives. Aging parents, unfortunately, simply get older, less capable, and less independent. Often, medical emergencies bring on the sudden need to care for elders, leaving us in confused emergency mode while furiously striving to adapt.

The dual caregiving burden hits women especially hard. According to the Alzheimer's Association, female caregivers may experience more depression and worse health than male caregivers, "because female caregivers tend to spend more time caregiving or on caregiving tasks, and to care for someone with greater cognitive, function and/or behavioral problems."[8]

Involving Your Teens

As parents of teens, this suffering is likely the last thing you want to validate, model, or pass on to children by example.

I spoke with Mickie Simon, a Washington, D.C.-based clinical social worker, on how to best manage the tricky bits of life in the panini generation while raising teens. She told me, "I believe that it is important for parents to start talking about life and death when kids are young. The trauma comes from avoiding the topic and living in a culture that resists aging and dying. Death is part of life, and even young kids can understand that every living thing has a life cycle."

Simon continued, "Parents today often avoid giving their teens responsibilities, saying they are too busy with extracurriculars or that

---

8 "Women and Alzheimer's," Alzheimer's Association. https://www.alz.org/alzheimers-dementia/what-is-alzheimers/women-and-alzheimer-s.

their schoolwork is more important. But teaching and modeling that we are all responsible to work together to make a family function should not be avoided. Then conversations about caregiving for aging parents are organic and can be part of the planning around how each member can contribute to helping the family run."

Of course, the panini generation should not look to their teens as primary support for themselves or for aging parents. But teenagers can and should contribute to this important responsibility.

Teens can step up and take on more responsibility for managing themselves and the household. For example, teens can make their own meals (or the family meal), coordinate their own rides, or add on to their regular chores. A teen who drives can pick up younger siblings, opening time and space for you to bring your ailing mom to her doctor's appointment. Actions like these can ease your burden, providing more time for caregiving. Plus, the additional responsibilities give your teens a sense of pride in contributing to the familial situation, all while developing their "adulting" skills.

Panini Role Model Andrea Bibbs

Andrea Bibbs left her family home in Toronto just out of college. She began a meteoric career in Atlanta, which continued to thrive through her marriage and birth of her two children. While she started without local family or friends, she quickly built a loving, supportive community of fellow expats.

As her parents aged, plans were made for them to leave Canada and join her family in Atlanta, but these never came to fruition. Her children and their needs continued to grow, as did her parents' challenges.

"I had the opportunity to try a new path, and I took it," Andrea said. That path was an exit from the endless demands of her career and a new start as an entrepreneur. She founded a business, June Dragonfly (junedragonfly.com). To Andrea, the newfound flexibility suddenly felt more valuable than the secure resources of her decades-long role at her former employer. "I have a cultural responsibility as the eldest daughter," she said. "My parents are Guyanese, and this is what is expected of me." The time had come, and "there was no plan B, nothing to manage a slip and fall or a health emergency so far away." And there was another layer. "I want my children to see my values in practice, understand what it means to love parents, to have an age-appropriate handle on aging and dying, which means an understanding that life is finite—that has not been simple or singular. It is an ongoing conversation, but [one] that my husband and I agree is essential." Running this business allows her to travel to her parents quite often and still get work done while back in Canada.

Andrea's children are involved in the care of their grandparents, each in their own way. One child researched a biography on his grandparents, and the other makes regular check-in calls. Andrea uses consistent conversations with her family to tackle the present as well as the future, and she feels positive about the ways in which she can lovingly, carefully parent through it all. "I am available for my kids in all of the most important ways. This is not something that can be skipped over."

• • • • •

Here is some advice for confronting your panini generation years, in which you are balancing parenting a teen with caring for aging family members.

Marshal External Resources

Dual care is very hard to do alone, relying only on your own resources. In fact, you will likely face an intense drain on many of your most valuable resources, such as money, time for self-care, work and career, personal endeavors, friendships, your spouse, sleep, and your ability to maintain your sense of humor.

The best thing a panini parent can do is build up their support system and healthy outlets for their stress. It's so important to connect with others in similar situations. Seek out groups of caregivers dealing with the same illnesses as your parent(s). For example, there is a robust Parkinson's group on Facebook. Find adults who are being pressed in many of the same ways you are. Fortunately—or not—these affinity groups are easy to find because there are so many people facing these daunting challenges. Further, friends, neighbors, coworkers, family members, and even employers can all be important supports for you, both emotionally and by helping in specific ways (e.g., driving, helping with food prep, offering flexible scheduling).

Model Best Practices

This is a perfect time to think about and share how you would like to age, including creating a clear and updated will or trust, as well as a central hub for essential information. For example, a couple I know had a very hard time arranging for care and managing the finances of one set of aging parents who, after denying the need for care for a long time, declined extremely quickly, both physically and cognitively. Once this couple got through this emergency, the next thing they did was get their affairs in order with an updated will, trust, power of attorney, and medical proxies. "After going through what we did, we resolved we would never put our son in the same circumstance," they said. There are several resources that can help you set up advance directives and share information, including the workbook *What Matters Most* or consulting an estate planning attorney.

By communicating with your teen throughout this process, you are modeling the importance of planning, as well as the value of supportive adult relationships. Your teen should learn that they do not have to carry burdens alone.

Be Emotionally Open While Maintaining Healthy Boundaries

While your teen is part of your inner circle, they are not someone with whom you should share all the details and frustrations you are dealing with. That's what friends, support groups, and spouses are for. However, teens can and should be aware of the stress and strain of caretaking. There are (at least) three generations in this circumstance. Keep this in mind as you identify what is best and for whom.

You should be honest with your teen about the joys and sorrows of caregiving for aging family members (while shielding them from some details, as appropriate). By sharing your feelings about your stress, worry, and sadness—as well as your happy memories—you model the ability to acknowledge that life is filled with loss and challenges but also beautiful moments. Teens should know that, even through hardships, their grandparents are a true gift. This is the practice of holding many truths at once, acknowledging change, and accepting what is.

Practice Self-Care

Providing hands-on and emotional care for two generations at once is hard work. That's why it is so important to spend at least some time caring for yourself. Simply put, you can only run on fumes for so long. Dedicating yourself to engaging in what you enjoy, like time with friends or a Pilates class, is an instant recharge. The gift of time alone to read or take a long walk listening to your favorite music is not an indulgence; it is essential. (See Chapter 9 for more on self-care.)

Plan Ahead, If You Still Have Time

Many panini caregivers are thrust into elder care unexpectedly because of a medical emergency. However, if your parents are still of sound body and mind, one of the smartest and kindest things you can do for everyone involved is to have the difficult talk with them about assets, access, wills, finances, and living expectations. They will likely resist, ducking and weaving to get out of this conversation, but you must stick with it. It's not easy to get aging parents to hand over the car keys, look at senior living facilities, and accept that they need help. If your siblings are around, involve them from the word go. Teamwork is so important. Recently, apps such as CareMobi have been developed to help caregivers compile information and coordinate care among family members and health care providers.

Circumstances will vary, and, of course, there will always be a wide range of outcomes. Be confident in the fact that the timing is never quite right, so do not wait to begin planning. An organized, proactive plan—or at least clarity about your and your parents' key values—will serve as a great start and make it far less likely that you will be caught off guard when the time comes to act.

• • • • •

Being a primary caregiver both to your teen and aging family members is an intense undertaking. The panini is hot, messy, and pressure-filled. Your ability to set yourself up for success, plan ahead, marshal resources, involve your teen, and attend to your own mental health will make all the difference in this phase of your life.

Chapter 9
SELF-CARE

Andy Pool, Ph.D. and Eden Pontz

For one mom, a typical morning meant getting up by 6 a.m., getting her family ready for their days, and then going off to work for a long shift that often extended well into the evening. She'd come home to cook dinner and tend to her husband's and teenage daughter's needs. Because of her daily grind, her family time was often corrupted by the unrelenting stress of her day. Instead of engaging with her daughter, she was often short with her. Her daughter would snap back, "Why are you always yelling at me and getting upset about things that aren't a big deal?" It strained their relationship. This mom wished she could get into a more productive and loving mindset with her daughter but couldn't find a way to get there.

Parenting is one of life's most rewarding roles but also among the most challenging, especially for working parents dealing with their kids' sometimes turbulent teenage years. Observing teens' growing independence and identity development can be thrilling. However, these years present a distinctive mix of challenges and opportunities. Parents of teens may encounter mood swings and the almost constant demand for emotional support, often brought on by the academic, social, and developmental challenges teens face.

For working parents, balancing career responsibilities with raising preteens and teenagers often leaves little time for self-care. But prioritizing personal well-being is vital, not just for the parent, but also for the family's overall health. This chapter examines why self-care is a fundamental aspect of effective parenting, the obstacles that frequently hinder parents from embracing it, and techniques to incorporate self-care into a busy schedule.

The Importance of Self-Care

When flying on an airplane, the flight attendant instructs that, in an emergency, parents should put on their oxygen masks before putting on their child's. In other words, it is helpful—not selfish—to take care of yourself. Only then can you take the best care of others. Many parents mistakenly believe that addressing their own needs is selfish, particularly during their children's crucial teenage years. In reality, the inverse is true: A parent who engages in self-care is more present, patient, and emotionally available for their children. Teens are observant. They learn to manage stress, relationships, and challenges by observing their parents. When parents prioritize self-care, they convey a strong message: Caring for oneself is integral to caring for others.

Additionally, adolescents are known for testing limits and showcasing strong emotions as they transition into adulthood. Parents neglecting their own needs may become overwhelmed, leading to burnout or reactive parenting. As this one dad reflects[9]:

> *Honestly, taking care of myself has been a low priority. I'm 45, overweight and don't exercise. My knees and back aren't great. There's always something more pressing to do, or I'm just stressed and exhausted from working and being the primary parent—and I*

---

9 From Behson, S.J. (2015). *The Working Dad's Survival Guide: How to Succeed at Work and at Home.* Motivational Press: Melbourne, Florida.

often feel like I'm falling behind. When I do get some time for myself, it's all I can do to crash on the couch with some mindless TV.

Self-care enables parents to recharge and sustain emotional stability, which is crucial for guiding their teens through this turbulent stage. In addition, stress, inadequate sleep, and poor nutrition can adversely impact a parent's emotional and physical health. Regular self-care practices such as exercise, adequate sleep, and relaxation can help ensure that parents are physically and emotionally equipped to handle their numerous responsibilities.

Barriers to Self-Care for Working Parents

Even though self-care is crucial, it often appears unattainable for busy parents. Many feel pressed for time amid work obligations, school drop-offs, extracurricular activities, and household duties. Single parents or those lacking a robust support network, like nearby extended family, often struggle even more to find time for themselves. Recognizing these barriers can help parents tackle them effectively.

Further, it's common for parents to prioritize their teen's needs and feel guilty for taking personal time or spending money on their own self-care. Cultural expectations sometimes glamorize self-sacrifice in parenting, reinforcing that good parents must consistently place their children first. If you feel this way, ask yourself:

- Do I deserve to feel better?
- Will others be hurt if I take time for myself?
- Will taking time for myself harm or help me?
- How will taking a break now make me more effective the rest of the day?

Understand that self-care is key to maintaining your mental and physical health, which allows you to be a stronger parent to your teen.

Self-care isn't selfish. Breaking this guilt-laden mindset involves practicing self-compassion, setting realistic goals, and treating yourself with the kindness you would offer a friend.

Strategies for Effective Self-Care

Here is a non-comprehensive list of strategies you can implement as you manage work and teen parenting.

Redefine Self-Care as a Daily Habit

Self-care doesn't need to be costly, complicated, or time intensive. It's about establishing habits that nurture your mind, body, and spirit. Even spending five minutes on deep breathing, stretching, or enjoying a quiet cup of tea are important micro-moments of care. If you can carve out time for more, do so, but recognize that even small self-care moments, built into your daily routine, can be effective.

For example, you can begin your day with a morning stretch at your bedside, a gratitude journal entry, and a healthy breakfast so that you leave for work feeling good. Throughout your workday, you can take mini-breaks for meditation or office chair yoga. Consider turning one-on-one meetings into "walk and talks" or integrating Tai Chi exercises at the end of meetings. You can actually take a lunch break, instead of eating at your desk while working, and use that time to catch up with coworkers or take a walk outside.

In the evenings, remember to wind down. Listen to a comedy podcast on your commute. Create a routine at home that could include family game time, walking the dog, or listening to your favorite music. Before bed, unplug and write down things you must tackle the next day to get them off your mind before going to sleep. Once self-care becomes a habit, it's easier to maintain, as the automatic part of our brains keeps us on track.

Set Boundaries and Schedules

It is imperative that self-care becomes a regularly scheduled part of your busy week. If you don't schedule and protect the time you need, distractions and interruptions will get in the way. Learning to say "no" is crucial for self-care. Boundaries protect your time and energy, allowing you to focus on what truly matters.

If you need three hours a week for exercise and two more for community service, you need to protect this self-care time the same way you would an important work meeting or family event. Your shared family and work calendars need to reflect your priorities. By communicating when you are unavailable, your family and/or coworkers can plan around your schedule. For example, to help meet his physical, social, and mental health needs, one dad joined a Monday night men's basketball league. Because it was a regularly scheduled activity, he and his family planned around it—his spouse made sure to get home from work before game time, and his teens were responsible for preparing dinner (his manager even knew not to email him on Monday nights).

Prioritize Sleep

Sleep is essential for overall health, yet it's often the first sacrifice for parents. According to the National Institutes of Health, almost one in three adults report inadequate sleep. Lack of sleep interferes with work, school, driving, and social functioning; reduces focus, learning, and empathy; and is associated with anxiety, depression, and a host of chronic health problems. It is often helpful to create a bedtime ritual by maintaining a regular sleep schedule, minimizing screen time before bed, and transforming your bedroom into a calming environment. Further, much of the advice below will also positively impact sleep.

Stay Physically Active

Physical activity elevates energy levels, enhances mood, alleviates stress, and is associated with better sleep. As Stephen Covey reminds us in his classic book, *The Seven Habits of Highly Effective People*:

> Most of us think we don't have enough time to exercise. What a distorted paradigm! We don't have time not to. We're talking about three to six hours a week, or a minimum of thirty minutes a day, every other day. That hardly seems an inordinate amount of time considering the tremendous benefits in terms of impact on the other 162-165 hours of the week.

Exercise gives you more energy to tackle the other 165 hours of your week and is the single best thing you can do for your long-term health. If you don't have long stretches of time available, remember that some exercise is always better than none. You can also turn exercise into family bonding time by, for example, hiking or biking with your teens.

Use Technology

Technology, such as computers, phones, apps, and wearables, can help you stay on top of your self-care routine. Apple watches, Oura Rings, and Fitbits count steps, monitor heart rates, and track sleep quality. You can use tech to set reminders to get up, move, take your pulse, and breathe to slow your heart rate. Of course, the opposite is true, too—turning off technology, especially social media and constant email notifications, better allows you to relax.

Nourish Yourself

Proper nutrition is vital for body and mind. Planning and preparing healthy meals ahead of time can streamline your week. A few hours on a Sunday afternoon with a slow cooker or lasagna pan means several home-cooked, healthy meals ready for quick reheating during busy weekdays, saving time, stress, and resorting to unhealthy fast food. Some families find delivery services such as Blue Apron or Hello Fresh to be helpful in encouraging them to eat healthy, home-cooked meals. Also, remember to keep a water bottle with you to stay hydrated, and that occasionally indulging in a favorite snack can be a form of self-care.

Cultivate Emotional Well-Being

Attending to your mental and emotional health is as essential as physical care, and there are many resources you can call on to help. For example, mindfulness apps like Headspace or Calm provide guided meditation sessions to help minimize stress, therapists or lifestyle coaches can provide valuable strategies for managing parenting and work-related stress, and regular journaling of your thoughts and feelings can enhance self-reflection and clarity.

Engage in Joyful Activities

Allocate time for hobbies that bring you happiness. Consider revisiting past interests—such as painting, gardening, or playing an instrument—or explore something new. Learning a new skill can be refreshing and an excellent way to recharge. These activities can also be done with friends, partners, or your teens, generating even more benefits. For example, one dad with a piano-playing teen took a refresher course to brush up on his long-neglected guitar skills so they could jam together on weekends. Relatedly, spending meaningful time with your family can rejuvenate you. Regular family traditions, such as game nights or Sunday brunches, give families consistent space to enjoy each other.

Involve your Teens

Why not make self-care a family affair? Talk with your teens about stress and its impact on health. Work together to define what self-care means to them. Ask them questions like, "What relaxes you?" or "What brings you joy?" Listen carefully, and use their answers to help establish self-care practices that will work for them.

Remind them that self-care doesn't have to cost money or look like what they see on social media. One parent told us her child has loved taking bubble baths since she was little and still does at 17 to help her chill out. Another said his son takes a whiff of vanilla extract to help relax him when he's studying for tests. Better yet, engage in self-care together—even simple acts like breathing, humming, singing, or walking make a difference, all while role-modeling its importance. Lastly, when you and your teen are in tune with each other's emotions, you become better at identifying each other's stress and can provide support.

Strengthen Your Support Network

You don't have to do it all by yourself. Reach out to friends, family, or neighbors for assistance with carpooling or babysitting. Join parenting groups, both online and in-person, to exchange experiences with fellow parents who can offer emotional backing and practical tips. For example, City Dads Group now operates in more than 40 U.S. cities, providing community around fatherhood. If you can't find a group like this—after all, there are far more support groups for new parents than there are for parents of teens—maybe you can start your own by reaching out to parents from work, your neighborhood, or your teen's school. If you co-parent, ensure open communication with your partner to carve out time for each other's self-care.

Know When to Ask for Help

Acknowledging when you need help is perfectly okay. Requesting assistance from family, friends, or coworkers is a sign of strength. It shows you understand your limits. Further, if feasible, consider hiring help like cleaners, tutors, or sitters to lessen your load so you have more time to care for yourself. If you're feeling overwhelmed, seek support from a therapist, counselor, or doctor.

Take Time to Celebrate

As you build your self-care habits, take the time to celebrate small wins. Did you get to bed early last night? Did you find time in your schedule to take a walk? Did you eat healthy? Acknowledge the steps you've taken to prioritize your health and well-being. As you recognize progress, offer yourself a little reward.

Happier You, Happier Family

Don't be surprised when prioritizing self-care for yourself positively impacts your family and others around you. When you're more physically and emotionally well, you open yourself up to building stronger relationships. Higher energy levels let you focus and perform more effectively at work and home. Further, by modeling self-care, you set a positive example for your family and encourage them to prioritize their emotional health and well-being. Your teens are watching.

Remember the mother from the opening example? Happily, she started taking control of her situation by practicing self-care. She prioritized getting more sleep, stopped saying yes to everyone at work, and created an exercise routine that helped her manage stress. Because of her attention to self-care, she was able to rise to her challenges without losing her cool and to improve her relationship with her daughter.

Part IV

THE ROLE OF MANAGERS AND WORKPLACES IN SUPPORTING PARENTS

Chapter 10
CREATING A FAMILY-FRIENDLY WORKPLACE CULTURE

Jennifer Sabatini Fraone

"When my kids were little, everyone at work wanted to hear about them and see pictures. My boss and coworkers were understanding about my needs for flexibility, and my employer had well-designed policies around parental leave and benefits. Now that my kids are teens, I still need the emotional and tangible support I once had at work, but there doesn't seem to be any for parents in my situation."

Does this sound familiar to you? If so, you are not alone.

And if you manage parents of teens and want to support them at work, here's some guidance on how to help.

Most of *Work-Family Ready* provides advice to parents on how they can rise to the dual challenge of succeeding at work while parenting teenagers. But managers and employers need to be part of the solution. This chapter focuses on what employers and managers can do to better support parents of teens and how parents can advocate for and access this support.

Why Should Workplaces Care About Parents of Teens?

There is a common misconception about just how difficult parenting teenagers can be, and employers often overlook the challenges that many of their employees face. Adolescence is different from early childhood, but it's not necessarily easier (and this stage can extend well into the 20s). Parenting teens while maintaining work and career demands is a challenge that may spill over into the workplace, negatively impacting the caregiver's physical and mental health. In fact, the 2023 Cleo Family Health Index found that, among all caregivers, parents of high school students had the lowest self-reports of health and well-being.

Mental and emotional stress outside the workplace can impact an individual's concentration, anxiety, self-esteem, confidence, and behavior toward colleagues. These negative effects can ripple out into the work environment, creating more stressful communications, relationships, and team dynamics, not to mention lowered productivity, employee burnout, absenteeism, and turnover.

Teens may not require the hands-on care and feeding of younger children, but they need their parents to be consistently available to them. Teens need rides to school and extracurricular activities, coordination of their multiple activities, and a great deal of logistical and emotional support. Teens can also find themselves in emergency situations. Even as they push parents away, teens need them. In fact, increased involvement of parents in teens' lives has been identified as a protective factor against risky behaviors and a predictor of good mental health.

What Managers Need to Know About the Work-Family Issues Facing Parents of Teens

In some cases, parents may downshift or leave the workforce altogether to be more present for their teens' needs. In other cases, understanding bosses and organizational cultures can make all the difference. Here's some information about what your employees who care for teenagers are facing.

Teens Require Emotional Support

Adolescents require less day-to-day physical support, but the psychological support they need from their parents often greatly increases. In today's world, teens deal with *a lot*, including the impact of social media, relationship challenges, pressure to excel in high school to get into a good college, issues around substance use and abuse, definition of gender identity, and alarmingly high levels of anxiety and depression, just to name a few concerns. In fact, according to a Pew Research Center report from 2024, 69% of U.S. parents agree that it's harder being a teenager today, with the leading reasons for this centering around technology (social media as #1), "more pressures and expectations," and the fact that "the world/country has changed in a bad way."[10] The emotional labor involved in navigating the teenage years can put parents at risk for burnout, which can make it increasingly difficult for them to focus at work.

Busy Teens Create Time Demands on Parents

As a parent, it's crucial to be available for your teen, whether that means a ride to and from practice with a snack in the car or a heartfelt talk late at night about a bullying experience. Parents need consistent time with their adolescents. Family meals, showing up to sports and school events, and leisure time together are so important. Pressure from employers to work long or unpredictable hours can make it difficult to commit to uninterrupted parenting time. Of course, parents may also need to be able to leave work at short notice to respond to an emergency.

---

10 "Why Many Parents and Teens Think It's Harder Being a Teen Today" by Michelle Faverio, Jeffrey Gottfried, Kaitlyn Radde, Chris Baronavski, and Sara Atske. Pew Research Center, August 27, 2024.

Every Situation Poses Different Challenges

Families who have teens with developmental disabilities, neurodivergence, complex medical issues, or gender dysphoria have a heightened level of managerial, mental, and emotional loads (see page 108 for recommended readings). These parents may be torn between their work and their need to attend to both the day-to-day management of these issues as well as the unexpected crises that arise.

In addition, many parents of teens find themselves in the sandwich generation, which means also caring for their own parents or other aging relatives (see Chapter 8). Financial challenges can have a significant impact on parental stress, particularly when looking ahead to funding a college education, managing the escalating costs of sports and other extracurricular activities, and keeping up with the latest technologies.

Parents Face Stigma and Lack of Support

While parents may proudly share baby pictures or drawings from their school-age children in their offices, we are less likely to hear parents discuss their teens at work. This is especially true when teens are experiencing struggles. Barbara Ellen, writing in *The Guardian* on parents who take career breaks in order to care for teens, says, "There's a huge social stigma attached to out-of-control or struggling teenagers." She says parents will "talk all day and night about colic or potty training," but this isn't the case for their "teenager's vile mouth, terrifying food disorder, or escalating weed habit." Parental shame can occur if a child is not meeting the impossible standards of today's Facebook-fueled life expectations.

These challenges mean that many parents of teens become "invisible caregivers" who do not disclose their care needs or caregiving responsibilities to their colleagues or managers. Employers can begin to change this situation by promoting available benefits for caregivers, bringing in experts to talk about teen development and challenges, encouraging employees to be more open about how caregiving impacts their work, and offering opportunities to connect with other parents experiencing the same life stage.

It is important to remember that men are also caregivers. Research from the Boston College Center for Work & Family found that dads desire to be more involved in their children's lives but don't always feel supported in being an active caregiver.

Creating a Family-Friendly Workplace Culture

So, with all of this in mind, how can organizations develop a culture that enables employees to attend to these new issues and challenges while staying engaged at work? What does a family-friendly workplace look like for parents of teens?

Leadership and Empathy

Leadership plays a central role in establishing a caring organizational culture that acknowledges parents' challenges. Leaders can set the tone by sharing their own stories—in person, in a blog, via video, or at a town hall meeting. They can openly self-identify as caregivers, which could involve being explicit about leaving early to care for a family member. Leaders demonstrating that caregiving and career success are not mutually exclusive can be especially impactful for fathers, who often feel stigmatized when accessing flexibility and other family-related benefits.

Leaders also need to encourage managers to be flexible and empathic in how they lead their teams. These actions lay the groundwork for a psychologically safe work environment in which employees feel they can share their challenges with the assurance that they will be listened to and respected without jeopardizing their career advancement.

Flexibility

Flexibility for parents of teens involves much more than remote work options or leaving early to shuttle kids to extracurriculars. Remote work, hybrid work, and the four-day workweek all have their place as potential solutions. However, ad hoc flexibility to attend to outside responsibilities is equally important. This "as needed" flexibility requires working with employees when they need an occasional afternoon away from the office for a school event, medical appointment, college visit, or teen emergency.

The key to flexibility is communication. Managers should be proactively checking in with employees, asking about their needs, and creatively seeking ways to determine whether work can be accomplished in a more flexible manner. For example, can the employee complete their work from home later at night without missing a deadline or disrupting the team's workflow? (See Chapter 11 for more on communication strategies.)

Providing specific time-off options, such as caregiver leave or mental health days, can help when employees face a crisis or need a period away to prevent burnout. Some are even requesting "teen-ternity leave," when parents, usually mothers, take an extended career break to be physically, mentally, and emotionally present for older children as they make their way through adolescent traumas, peer pressures, exam stresses, etc.

Focus on Well-Being and Mental Health

Mental health was a growing concern before the COVID pandemic, but now it has become critical for organizations to address. Thankfully, many organizations are investing more in this crucial area, promoting the use of employee assistance programs (EAPs) and behavioral health services for employees and their families, offering workshops on mindfulness or self-care, and adding digital solutions for care management, counseling, and coaching. Promoting a culture of acceptance around mental health may include training well-being ambassadors throughout an organization and other efforts to increase empathy and decrease stigma.

Ensure access to mental health providers with expertise in adolescence when vetting new EAPs or digital mental health partners. These mental health supports are especially important for employees who need to be emotionally available for their teens. Research from the Institute for Family Studies found that the most important factor in the mental health of adolescents is the quality of their relationships with their caregivers. Children in a high-quality relationship with their parents are much less likely to show signs of depression, anxiety, or suicidal ideation and generally exhibit behaviors associated with positive social development. Moreover, these benefits predict stronger mental health decades into the future. Employers who help support strong parent-teen relationships will gain the gratitude and loyalty of their employees.

Family-Friendly Benefits

While new parents are often offered a full suite of benefits and services, employer support may diminish by the teen years—but it doesn't have to. In addition to inclusive health care and mental health benefits for the entire family—employees and their dependents—there are several other benefits that can be particularly helpful for parents of teens. For instance, educational support and resources are highly valued by parents of teens. These can include tutoring or homework help services, connection with specialized extracurricular activities or camps, and access to coaching to help teens and their parents navigate the college application process.

Financial Support

Parenting teenagers can be expensive, and many families are feeling financially squeezed. Employers can respond with an array of solutions to support financial well-being, such as free tutoring services or flexible contributions that can be used to pay for summer camps and enrichment programs. Financial planning services and counseling, dependent care flexible spending accounts, and employer-subsidized 529 plan contributions can all help alleviate financial stress. Of course, paying livable wages is the most direct way to support all employees, including parents staring down college tuition bills.

Community

The need for community and connection cannot be overstated in this era in which loneliness at work is pervasive. Unlike the fellowship that often accompanies parenting younger kids, such as "mommy and me" classes and frequent elementary school events, parental camaraderie is often lacking during the teen years, leading to a sense of isolation. Employers can help fill this gap by convening a forum where parents of teens can find validation for what they are going through, bounce ideas off one another, share resources, and learn more about the supports that the company offers.

Such connections can be facilitated through employee resource groups (ERGs), affinity groups, lunch and learns, or community boards where parents can share ideas. In a large company, consider breaking the caregiver ERG into subgroups or host events based on who your employees are caring for (new babies, young children, teens, elders, spouses, persons with special needs). This can be one of the lowest cost, highest impact approaches to helping parents feel a sense of belonging in the workplace and develop new coping strategies.

> ### Evaluating Your Workplace: Is It Work-Family Ready?
>
> 1. Does my manager/team have empathy for my family situation and understand my need for flex hours for events/appointments?
>
> 2. Do my company's employee benefits include mental health services, educational support, and parent coaching that can help address the comprehensive needs of teenage dependents?
>
> 3. Does my employer have a family/caregiver ERG and, if so, are there specific activities/subgroups to provide community and support to parents of teens?
>
> If the answer to any or all these questions is no, consider ways you might be able to become an agent for change, advocating for yourself and other parents.

Closing Advice

Maintaining employment and advancing a career while parenting teens can be a challenge. Family-friendly organizations should lead the way by increasing managers' awareness of the nuances of this life phase and preparing them to have productive and supportive conversations with their employees. Employers should offer a broad range of family-related benefits and programs designed for parents of teens. Managers should point parents to available benefits, resources, and leave and respond to requests with empathy and compassion. Taken together, these efforts to support families through a complicated phase of life will engender employee loyalty and engagement.

Recommended Reading

Susan M. Sawyer, Peter S. Azzopardi, Dakshitha Wickremarathne, and George C. Patton, "The Age of Adolescence," *Lancet Journal of Child and Adolescent Health* 2, no. 3 (March 2018): 223–228.

Gretchen Gavett, "Your Employees Are Also Caregivers. Here's How to Support Them," *Harvard Business Review*, November 13, 2024.

Michelle Faverio, Jeffrey Gottfried, Kaitlyn Radde, Chris Baronavski, and Sara Atske, "Why Many Parents and Teens Think It's Harder Being a Teen Today," Pew Research Center, August 27, 2024.

Brad Harrington, Jennifer Sabatini Fraone, and Jegoo Lee, *The New Dad: The Career-Caregiving Conflict* (Boston College, 2017).

Jonathan Rothwell, "The Quality of Parent-Child Relationships in U.S. Families," Gallup, January 10, 2024.

Jonathan Rothwell, "Parenting Is the Key to Adolescent Mental Health," Institute for Family Studies, blog post, November 30, 2023.

"Working While Parenting a Teen: Not What I Expected," *Women at Work* (podcast), *Harvard Business Review*, November 18, 2024.

ACT for Youth, "Youth Statistics: Family Structure and Relationships," updated February 9, 2024.

Melissa Willets, "Why Parents Are Choosing to Leave Work When Their Children Become Teenagers," *Parents*, November 30, 2023.

Barbara Ellen, "Is 'Teen-ternity' Leave Just a New Way to Make Mothers Feel Guilty?" *The Guardian*, November 26, 2023.

Chapter 11

MANAGER-EMPLOYEE COMMUNICATION STRATEGIES

Supporting Parents of Teenagers in the Workplace

Amy Beacom, Ed.D.

Picture this: Your team member is in the middle of presenting to a key client when their phone buzzes with a call from their teenager's school. You watch them hesitate, their eyes darting between the phone and the screen, knowing they're caught in an impossible choice. As their manager, what you do next matters more than you might think.

If you're managing parents of teenagers, scenarios like this aren't the exception—they're increasingly becoming the rule. While organizations have made strides in supporting expecting and new parents navigating parental leave and return, they're often less prepared for the unique challenges faced by parents of teenagers. Yet these challenges can be just as demanding and often more emotionally complex than those faced by parents of younger children.

Additionally, for many parents the teen years bring up intense awareness that their child's time at home is coming to an end. They will be moving off to their own life soon. This can be very emotional for parents and, for many, it increases their desire to be present and available for their teenagers as much as possible, which increases tension between work and home demands.

How you communicate with your direct reports around their parenting responsibilities can help make this phase of their personal and professional life something they can progress and thrive through or, alternatively, a time that forces them out of the workplace altogether.

Understanding What Your Employees Are Facing

Parenting teenagers today is fundamentally different than it was 10 years ago when smartphones and social media were new, or even five years ago before the pandemic altered their experiences. The challenges faced today are less predictable and often more intense—and it doesn't look like that is going to improve anytime soon. Also, parenting teenagers while maintaining a career is fundamentally different from parenting younger children. I've had many clients cite this maxim: "Little kids, little problems. Big kids, big problems." Consider these all-too-common scenarios:

- Your employee's 15-year-old is struggling with depression and has recently attempted suicide. They need twice-weekly therapy appointments during work hours.

- Your employee's teen calls them in the middle of the afternoon, frantic after getting into a fender-bender. No one is hurt, but the teen doesn't know what to do next.

- Your employee needs to visit multiple colleges with their high school junior, requiring several extended weekends

away; they know senior year will bring months of college application support and more visits.
- Your employee discovers their child has been targeted in a sexploitation scam through their social media use; police intervention is followed by psychological support.

These situations share three key characteristics: They're emotionally charged, they often arise without warning (or with short notice), and they require flexible, immediate, and often ongoing responses.

Research shows that, while the scheduling demands posed by teens might be less rigid than those for younger children, the emotional intensity and unpredictability of teenage-related challenges can be significantly higher. This reality necessitates a more nuanced approach to communication and management.

Building Psychological Safety Through Communication

The foundation for effectively supporting your direct reports who have teenagers is trust, built through consistent, thoughtful communication. Sincerely communicated emotional support from supervisors is crucial for employee well-being and performance. The paragraphs below show how to put this into practice.

Creating psychological safety isn't just about having an open-door policy. It's about consistently demonstrating through your actions that your employees can trust talking to you about their challenges, whether those are coming from work or home. Through your words and actions as a manager, you can actively build a team climate where parents feel secure having a professional discussion about sensitive matters regarding their teenagers without fear of judgment or consequences. Your efforts to create this type of work-family supportive environment will also benefit all employees.

Start by being impeccable with confidentiality. This means more than just keeping secrets—it means absolutely refusing to participate in office gossip, even seemingly harmless conversations about why someone might be working remotely or leaving early. Indeed, if you see this happening, your role is to step in and advocate for your direct report and course-correct the conversation to align with the culture you want to create. When employees see that you never discuss other team members with negativity, they'll feel more confident sharing their own challenges with you.

Consistency is also crucial for psychological safety. Your decision to provide a supportive response shouldn't depend on whether you're having a good day or if your employee just landed a big client. When team members see that you respond with the same level of understanding in all situations—whether your top performer needs to leave early for their child's therapy appointment or your new hire for their teen's soccer championship—they learn they can count on your support regardless of the time, day, or circumstance.

Of course, there may be times when what you need from your direct report for work conflicts with what they need for home. For example, let's say you have a project deadline at noon on Thursday, and your employee unexpectedly needs to leave early while you are finalizing plans on Wednesday afternoon. In cases like this, direct communication is key. You could say, "I completely understand that you need to head out early today and, as you know, we do have our project deadline tomorrow. I want to make sure that both can happen. Do you have any creative solutions that can get both needs met?" They might do the work later that night, you might bring in another team member, you might both come in early the next day, or you might see if you can extend the deadline. Coming up with the solution together lets them know that you support them and that their needs matter.

Implement Regular Check-Ins

Regular communication is crucial when supporting parents of teenagers, but it's not just about having more meetings. It's about creating touchpoints that build trust and allow for proactive problem-solving. The key is to establish a rhythm of communication that feels supportive rather than surveillance-like and creates space for both immediate needs and longer-term planning.

Monthly Work-Life Integration Conversations

Monthly conversations focusing on work-life integration work best when they're structured but flexible. One manager I worked with, James, developed a simple framework that helped guide these discussions without making them feel rigid. He said, "I start each monthly check-in with Camilla, whose son is struggling with anxiety, by simply asking, 'How are things going with balancing everything right now?' Then we explore what's working well, what challenges she anticipates in the coming months, and what adjustments might help. It's amazing how often we can head off potential conflicts just by having these conversations in advance."

These conversations should feel collaborative rather than administrative. For example, instead of asking, "Do you need any schedule changes next month?", try, "Let's look ahead to next month and see how we can set both you and the team up for success."

Weekly Quick-Connects

While monthly check-ins provide a strategic overview, weekly quick-connects help address immediate needs and maintain ongoing support. These shorter touchpoints shouldn't feel like another obligation. They're meant to be brief, practical conversations that help both manager and employee stay aligned and agile in their response to emerging situations.

Think of these quick-connects as pressure-release valves. They give your direct report regular opportunities to raise concerns before they become crises. For instance, one parent might mention during a quick-connect that their teenager has been struggling to adjust to their ADHD medicine, and it's profoundly impacting their sleep. This early heads-up allows you to start thinking about flexibility options, even if it is only in your own mind, before it becomes an emergency where their teen refuses or is unable to go to school.

Create and Communicate Clear Emergency Response Protocols

Having clear communication protocols for different types of situations is essential. Through my work with organizations, I've found that emergencies involving teenagers typically fall into three categories:

1. **Immediate response required:** These are situations where your employee needs to drop everything immediately. Think suicide threats, medical emergencies, or serious accidents. One manager shared this experience: "When Quincy got the call that his son was having a mental health crisis at school, he didn't need to think about protocol—he knew he could leave immediately and contact me when he was able. That pre-established understanding made a critical difference in his ability to respond to his son's needs."

2. **Same-day response needed:** These situations require attention within hours but may allow for some work transition time. Examples include school disciplinary meetings, unexpected after-school events that require a parent chauffeur, or interpersonal incidents that need parent intervention.

3. **Flexible response timing:** These are important but plannable events like college visits, routine medical appointments, or school meetings. While they need attention, they allow for more coordinated advance planning.

Create simple communication systems for each type. One team uses a straightforward text-based system: "911" for immediate emergencies, "Urgent" for same-day needs, and "Heads up" for situations requiring attention but not immediate response. This clarity helps reduce employee stress about how to communicate in crisis moments.

Model Effective Communication

One of the most powerful tools you have as a manager is your own experience. Sharing appropriate examples from your work-life challenges—whether you're raising teenagers yourself or caring for aging parents (or both!)—helps normalize these conversations. For instance, you might say, "I remember when my daughter was applying to colleges. Those campus visits seemed to pop up at the most inconvenient times, but I'm so glad I made them a priority." This kind of authentic sharing sends a clear message: "Everyone juggles caregiving responsibilities and work, and I support you."

Perhaps most importantly, demonstrate through both your words and actions that using flexible work arrangements won't derail your direct report's career. This means more than just saying you support flexibility—it means actively modeling it yourself. When you openly adjust your own schedule for family commitments, like publicly announcing in your out-of-office message that you are leaving work early for your child's doctor appointment or letting the full team know you are taking a work-from-home day when your teenager is struggling, you show your team that these aren't just policies on paper—they're real options that successful professionals use to integrate work and family responsibilities.

Signs Your Communication Strategy Is Working

Effective communication strategies ripple throughout your team. Here are key indicators that your approach is succeeding, along with specific examples of what success looks like in practice:

1. **Employees feel comfortable discussing family needs and proposing solutions.** Rather than hiding challenges or apologizing for them, you'll see team members confidently presenting thought-out proposals. One employee mapped out her entire college tour schedule, identified coverage needs, and created detailed handoff documents before approaching her manager for discussion.

2. **Crisis situations are handled smoothly with minimal disruption.** When one employee had to suddenly leave due to their teenager's mental health crisis, three different team members stepped up to seamlessly divide his presentation responsibilities without needing management intervention.

3. **The team proactively demonstrates empathy and problem-solving creativity.** This could look like proactively scheduling meetings around known teen-support appointment times, creating shared calendars, or suggesting innovative solutions to work coverage. One team started offering "flex blocks," where members could temporarily reduce their workload during intensive parenting periods, knowing others would do the same for them when needed.

4. **Work-life discussions become normalized as part of your team culture.** You might overhear conversations like, "I've got backup coverage tomorrow afternoon—do you need me to shift any of our deadlines?" rather than detailed personal discussions.

When your communication strategy is working, you'll notice that discussions about work-life integration shift from being crisis-driven to purpose-driven. Instead of constantly putting out fires, your team spends more time proactively planning and supporting each other. This creates a more sustainable, resilient workplace for everyone, regardless of their family situation or where they are in their working parent journey.

Creating Sustainable Communication Systems

Supporting employees who are parents of teenagers requires thoughtful, proactive communication strategies that recognize the unique challenges these parents face. Remember these key principles:

- **Trust is foundational.** Your consistent demonstration of support, understanding, and confidentiality creates the foundation for effective work-life integration.
- **Clarity enables flexibility.** Clear communication structures and protocols enable greater adaptability for accommodations when challenges arise.
- **Team communication matters.** When you effectively support parents through good communication, you create a more resilient, adaptable workplace culture that benefits everyone.

The journey of supporting working parents with teens while maintaining high performance standards isn't always easy, but with thoughtful communication strategies, you can create an environment where everyone can thrive.

Conclusion

Thank you so much for reading *Work-Life Ready*. We hope you found the book to be an enjoyable and helpful guide for you as you rise to the challenge of parenting your teenager, succeeding in your career, and maintaining your well-being. As a recap and review, here are a few key lessons from each chapter.

Chapter 1: How Does Having a Teen Change You?

Move from manager to consultant, relinquishing some control and trusting your teen to make decisions and learn from their mistakes.

Balance autonomy and boundaries by creating open communication and collaborative rule-setting to establish mutual respect and trust.

Emphasize emotional support by listening without judgment, validating emotions, and remaining calm.

Seek support when needed, whether from extended family, school counselors, coaches, clergy, or doctors.

Chapter 2: How Does Having a Teen Change Your Household?

Create a family contract for what you expect of your teen (e.g., chores, good grades, avoiding trouble, being home by curfew) and what they can expect from you in return (e.g., allowance, paying for things, gradually increasing independence).

Create a teen-related budget and distinguish between high-priority items and lower-priority ones.

Use a shared family calendar app and schedule a weekly planning session to review everyone's commitments.

Set clear rules around driving privileges and expectations and work together to manage the logistics.

Chapter 3: How Does Having a Teen Affect Your Work?

Manage time and energy: Understanding that energy—not just time—is a crucial resource revolutionizes how you approach your workday.

Implement the triple win by evaluating and navigating situations through three essential lenses: benefit to you, benefit to your work quality, and benefit to others you work with.

Apply your leadership expertise by delegating and knowing when to seek help both at home and work.

Model work-life integration, involving your teen in discussions and sharing your decision-making process openly.

Chapter 4: Setting Boundaries at Home to Accommodate Work

Communicate and cocreate boundaries with your teen to help calibrate expectations and decrease interruptions by having conversations about when, how, and under what circumstances they can reach you when you are at work.

Preserve certain times for parenting, yet watch them from a distance so that you notice signs of distress or poor decision-making, while also giving them the space they need to develop.

Model healthy work-life balance: By showing them how to block time for work and family, they can learn how to block time for schoolwork, jobs, and busy social lives.

Chapter 5: Aligning with Your Co-Parent for Effective Family Management

Understand your core values as individuals and as a family to help you prioritize what's most important and simplify decision-making.

Communicate proactively: By digging a bit deeper to talk about what you care about most, you open doors for more effective communication and problem resolution.

Experiment together as a family: By starting with your core values and considering the reality of your current lives, try an experiment to help you address a parenting challenge.

Chapter 6: Partnering with Your Teen

Create a fair and just household management plan, using family composition as a useful framework to start.

Exhibit positive role-modeling behaviors to teach teens about the value of shared responsibility in the home, keeping the household operating smoothly, caring for family members, and creating a positive emotional climate through teamwork.

Empower your teen to actively participate in how their household runs to foster their sense of self and belonging.

Express empathy and use teamwork when your teen is experiencing conflict among school, work, family, and/or other roles by validating and empathizing with your teen's feelings of overwhelm.

Chapter 7: Setting Boundaries at Work to Accommodate Your Family

Delegate effectively to become a better leader and parent.

Define what is and is not an emergency by being proactive about letting people know what they are empowered to resolve in your absence, as well as what requires your involvement.

Communicate your UN-availability—it is vital for our well-being to set boundaries at work to accommodate family.

Pay yourself first by establishing the three things you absolutely must do each day for your well-being.

Chapter 8: The Panini Generation: Balancing Parenting Teens and Other Caregiving Responsibilities

Involve your teen: They can step up and take on more responsibility for managing themselves and the household.

Marshal external resources to build up the support system you'll need to provide care for aging family members while also being a present parent and to find healthy outlets for your stress.

Model best practices by thinking about and sharing how you would like to age—and then proactively put a plan in place.

Be emotionally open while maintaining healthy boundaries by being honest with your teen about the joys and sorrows of caregiving for aging family members.

Chapter 9: Self-Care

Redefine self-care as a daily habit to establish routines that nurture your mind, body, and spirit. Build in and protect time in your weekly calendar for important self-care activities, ensuring that family and work respect these boundaries. Enlist the help of others, including your teen, to ensure you get the time you need.

Prioritize sleep by creating a bedtime ritual.

Stay physically active—it's the single best thing you can do for your long-term health—and consider preparing healthy meals ahead of time to streamline your week.

Engage in joyful activities by allocating time for hobbies that bring you happiness, perhaps even involving your teens in your care activities.

Chapter 10: Creating a Family-Friendly Workplace Culture

Leaders should set an empathetic tone to establish a caring organizational culture that acknowledges parents' challenges.

Communicate flexibility by checking in with employees, asking about their needs, and creatively seeking ways to determine whether work can be accomplished in a more flexible manner.

Focus on well-being and mental health by promoting a culture of acceptance around mental health and offering services and workshops.

Create community to help parents feel a sense of belonging in the workplace and develop new coping strategies.

Chapter 11: Manager-Employee Communication Strategies: Supporting Parents of Teenagers in the Workplace

Understand what your employees are facing as the emotional intensity and unpredictability of teenage-related challenges can be especially difficult for your employees to navigate.

Build psychological safety through communication by consistently demonstrating that your employees can talk to you about their challenges, whether those are coming from work or home.

Model effective communication by sharing appropriate examples from your own work-life challenges.

· · · · ·

Finally, as editor, I'd like to add my own last piece of advice.

Teenagers are amazing! It is a privilege to be a parent of a teenager. Helping them grow into independent adults, even with all the inevitable ups and downs, twists and turns, and highs and lows, is a joy. Yes, this developmental stage is often difficult for both teens and parents, but it is also extremely rewarding.

Perhaps the best way to navigate our parenting journeys is to start from a place of empathy for the dizzying array of changes—physical, emotional, social—your teen is facing. Empathy requires listening without judgment and seeing things from your teen's perspective. Only then can we most effectively work with them to provide the right balance of guidance and independence, help them with their challenges, and find the right balance for ourselves as we attend to all the roles in our busy lives.